Harmful Sexual Behaviour in Young Children and Pre-Teens

There has been considerable research and authorship on child sexual abuse; however, much of this research has focused on adult perpetrators and child victims. Less attention has been paid to children's harmful sexual behaviour and the multitude of influences.

Harmful Sexual Behaviour in Young Children and Pre-Teens provides evidence-based understanding on typical sexual development versus harmful sexual behaviour; the prevalence and impacts associated with harmful sexual behaviour; Australian laws, policies, and educator responsibilities; responses and support systems for children who display harmful sexual behaviour; and the implications and challenges for future practice. This book provides understandings that directly respond to the recent Australian Royal Commission into Institutional Responses to Child Sexual Abuse recommendation 10.1 to address (a) primary prevention strategies to educate family, community members, carers, and professionals about preventing harmful sexual behaviours, (b) secondary prevention strategies to ensure early intervention when harmful sexual behaviours are developing, and (c) tertiary intervention strategies to address harmful sexual behaviours.

The authors present a review of psychological, sociological, legal, and educational research to inform and support professionals involved in the wellbeing and education of children to understand, manage, and reduce harmful sexual development in children.

Lesley-anne Ey, BECE (Hons) PhD, is Senior Lecturer in Education Futures at the University of South Australia with expertise in children's harmful sexual behaviours, the impact of media on children's socio-sexual development, bullying, and child protection issues, with the aim to support teachers and inform curriculum.

Elspeth McInnes AM, BA (Hons 1) PhD, is Associate Professor in Education Futures at the University of South Australia with expertise in issues of child abuse and child protection, family violence, trauma and child development, and public policy regarding family law, income support, and family services.

Harmful Sexual Behaviour in Young Children and Pre-Teens
An Education Issue

Lesley-anne Ey and
Elspeth McInnes

First published 2020
by Routledge
2 Park Square, Milton Park, Abingdon, Oxon OX14 4RN

and by Routledge
52 Vanderbilt Avenue, New York, NY 10017

Routledge is an imprint of the Taylor & Francis Group, an informa business

© 2020 Lesley-anne Ey and Elspeth McInnes

The right of Lesley-anne Ey and Elspeth McInnes to be identified as authors of this work has been asserted by them in accordance with sections 77 and 78 of the Copyright, Designs and Patents Act 1988.

All rights reserved. No part of this book may be reprinted or reproduced or utilised in any form or by any electronic, mechanical, or other means, now known or hereafter invented, including photocopying and recording, or in any information storage or retrieval system, without permission in writing from the publishers.

Trademark notice: Product or corporate names may be trademarks or registered trademarks, and are used only for identification and explanation without intent to infringe.

British Library Cataloguing-in-Publication Data
A catalogue record for this book is available from the British Library

Library of Congress Cataloging-in-Publication Data
A catalog record for this book has been requested

ISBN: 978-0-367-02286-0 (hbk)
ISBN: 978-0-367-49921-1 (pbk)
ISBN: 978-0-429-40045-2 (ebk)

Typeset in Times New Roman
by Apex CoVantage, LLC

Contents

1 **Introduction**   1

   The problem at hand and purpose of the book 1
   Historical influences on the construction of children
     as sexual beings 2
   Children's displays of sexual behaviour: attitudes
     and influences 4
   Overview of the chapters 6
   References 8

2 **Typical sexual development and harmful sexual behaviour**   12

   Introduction 12
   Children's typical sexual development 13
   Physiological sexual development 15
   Defining harmful sexual behaviour: exploring
     the language 16
   Conclusion 19
   References 20

3 **Children's harmful sexual behaviour: a global phenomenon?**   23

   Introduction 23
   Prevalence of harmful sexual behaviour 25
   Prevalence of harmful sexual behaviour in Australia and the
     context where it occurs 29
   Harmful sexual behaviour in education settings: preschools,
     schools, and out-of-school care 30

vi Contents

Conclusion 31
References 32

4 Aftermath and impacts of harmful sexual behaviour 38

Introduction 38
Impacts of harmful sexual behaviour for children who have
    experienced unwanted sexual encounters 38
Trauma 39
Mental health 41
Interpersonal relationships 41
Sexual identity 42
Physical health 42
Education, employment, and economic security 43
Impacts of harmful sexual behaviour for children who display
    the behaviour 45
Conclusion 46
References 46

5 Influences on harmful sexual behaviour: child
  characteristics, familial and social context 49

Introduction 49
Victims of abuse 51
Family context 53
Children with an intellectual disability 54
Media 55
Pornography 56
Conclusion 57
References 57

6 Laws and responsibilities 61

Introduction 61
Sexual behaviours involving children and Australian laws 61
Legal age and culpability of sexual behaviour: Australian
    states and territories 63
The problem with family law in Australia 64
Laws guiding school policies on harmful sexual
    behaviour 65

Contents vii

Ongoing duty of care 66
Conclusion 67
References 68

7 **Educator knowledge of harmful sexual behaviour and their training needs** 71

Introduction 71
Educators' understanding of developmentally normal and harmful sexual behaviour 72
Educators' views of typical sexual behaviour of children with whom they are currently working 73
Educators' views of harmful sexual behaviour of children with whom they are currently working 74
Current training for educators 75
Educators' training in identifying and responding to children displaying sexual behaviour 78
What educators want 78
A move to a national approach 79
Conclusion 80
References 80

8 **Responding to and supporting children who display harmful sexual behaviour: an educator's approach** 83

Introduction 83
Therapeutic treatment for children who display harmful sexual behaviour 84
External support services for children who have harmful sexual behaviour 85
Initial responses 86
Long-term responses 87
Behaviour support plan 88
Support and safety plan 88
Individual educators' support strategies 89
Whole-school responses 93
Conclusion 95
References 95

9 Identifying challenges and prevention strategies 98

Introduction 98
Revisiting children's vulnerabilities through an ecological systems approach 99
Challenges from media and technologies 104
Training for educators and other professionals 106
Child and family education 107
Decreasing the physical context risk: physical setting and design 109
Conclusion 110
References 111

10 Conclusion 115

Introduction 115
Increased numbers of children experiencing maltreatment 116
Increased numbers of children attending formal child care 117
Public inquiries into child protection systems and child sexual abuse 118
Rapid growth in pornography and child exploitation material online 123
What's to be done? 124
References 129

Index 134

1 Introduction

The problem at hand and purpose of the book

Children's displays of harmful sexual behaviour in education settings is a relatively new phenomenon. Its emergence has thrust educators and education departments into a position in which they must respond appropriately and effectively to support the child and other affected children, whilst also preventing the problem from recurring or escalating. So far, there has been only limited research into children's harmful sexual behaviour, particularly in educational settings. This book draws on national and international research to examine the prevalence of harmful sexual behaviour, before looking at the evidence-based risks and impacts of harmful sexual behaviour on younger children. It then moves to highlight Australian educators' legal and professional responsibilities towards children. Educators' understanding in this area is essential for them to work collaboratively with children, their families, and health professionals to support all children, whilst positioning children's wellbeing and education at the forefront of their practice. Early detection and timely intervention are imperative in order to support children and reduce potential impacts. This book draws on psychological, sociological, legal, and educational perspectives to support professionals involved in the wellbeing and education of children to understand, manage, and reduce dysfunctional sexual development in young children.

This introductory chapter begins by discussing historical perspectives of 'childhood innocence' before moving to the contemporary understanding that children are sexual beings. It discusses attitudes about children's displays of sexual behaviour, cultural change, and the social issues that play a role in the rise of harmful sexual behaviour. It provides a brief description of the problem at hand and the need for this book for educators and other professionals whose work involves supporting the wellbeing of children. It then provides a brief outline of each of the chapters.

2 *Introduction*

Historical influences on the construction of children as sexual beings

Over the centuries, changes in ideologies, economies, and technology have affected considerable shifts in how children and childhood have been viewed. As far back as records have been retained, there have been debates and differences in beliefs about children and childhood. Views expressed by social historian Philippe Ariès suggest that 'childhood' was a social construct that developed in the late seventeenth century. Before the 1800s, children older than 7 years were seen as miniature adults (Archard 1993; Bullough 2004). This view was reflected in dress codes and expectations for children to contribute to the family and the economy (Slee & Schute 2003).

Western perspectives on children as sexual beings have shifted throughout the centuries. These have been largely influenced by life expectancy, views surrounding puberty and entry to reproductive adulthood, and attitudes regarding the protection of children. Since the nineteenth century, childhood has been redefined into extended phases, to protect childhood as a period exempt from adult roles, including reproduction and paid work. Pre-pubescent children have not been conventionally viewed as sexual beings since the 1200s (Bullough 2004; Levin & Kilbourne 2008). Before the thirteenth century, children could be betrothed from age 7 as they were considered proficient in expressing themselves at that age. During the latter half of the thirteenth century, betrothal as a binding act of marriage was negated if it had not been consummated by the age of 12 years (Bullough 2004). From the fourteenth century through to the sixteenth century, children were sexually sought after for marriage and prostitution: virgin girls aged 12–13 were particularly in demand. During the seventeenth century, public outrage at the sexual exploitation of children grew, and subsequently the age of consent was gradually raised from 10 to 16 years (Bullough 2004). By the Victorian period in the nineteenth century, Western culture and science predominantly viewed sexual development as commencing with puberty, which was considered a single event or developmental milestone (Worthman, Plotsky, Schechter, & Cummings 2010). Owing to the influence of Romanticism, the nineteenth century saw a shift in public views of children towards seeing them as innately good, pure, and innocent (Cunningham 2005), as well as asexual (Archard 1993). The Victorians emphasised the preservation of childhood and attempted to protect children from adult matters, including information about sex (Bullough 2004).

These views prevailed at the time of Australian colonisation. Interest in children's wellbeing and rights was rising, and childhood was largely seen as a state of innocence (Darian-Smith 2010). This perspective dominates contemporary views, with children being seen as needing support and protection: 'Girls, in particular, were seen as vulnerable and in need of protection because of their sexuality' (Darian-Smith 2010, p. 4). During the nineteenth and early twentieth centuries, any form of sex education or discussion about sex or sexuality was withheld from children, with the aim of upholding childhood innocence and to protect them from immorality. The introduction of sex education for children was initially directed at Christian mothers to provide them with the resources to impart accurate information about sex to their children (aged over 12 years). This practice controlled what information children would receive, whilst also imparting moral conventions. For example, children were taught that to engage in any form of sexual activity before wedlock was dirty and disorderly (Swain, Warne, & Hillel 2004).

Sex education or discussion about sexuality was very much a private affair and was only addressed in the family home. Before World War I, sex education advocates pressured Australian governments to provide sex education to children in secondary schools, but such education was denied on grounds of protecting childhood innocence and fears that providing such education may introduce children to sex prematurely, and thus potentially corrupt them. After World War I, an increase in venereal disease resulted in more births of deformed babies and inspired further debate. There was a general acknowledgement that children entering puberty needed formal sex education; however, there was disagreement about what should be taught and by whom. Medical, educational, and Christian leaders proposed several approaches, including education about personal hygiene of the sexual organs, reproduction, moral training, and abstinence; however, there was no general consensus. In the 1930s, primary responsibility for children's sex education shifted from mothers to public education programs, including secondary schools (Swain et al. 2004).

The rise of child development as a sub-discipline of psychology began with Charles Darwin. This generated an increase in research about child development (Parke & Gauvain 2009), including children's sexual development, beyond strictly physiological perspectives (Freud 2014). Contemporary research has drawn on adults' memories of their own sexual behaviour as children, parents' and teachers' observations of children's sexual behaviour, and observations of children who present with concerning or harmful sexual behaviour (Staiger 2005). From such research, it has been widely recognised by child development professionals that sexual development and expression begin at infancy (Levin & Kilbourne 2008). In fact, according to DeLamater and Friedrich (2002), sexual reactions are present from birth. Despite such understanding, there is no universal consensus about what typical or harmful sexual behaviour is. Nevertheless,

4 *Introduction*

there are some key concepts thought to indicate healthy and natural sexual expression. For example, very young children's sexual behaviour is commonly explorative and driven by curiosity. Sexual play in childhood appears to be an information-gathering process in which there is mutual exploration and agreement. Children engaging in sexual play are typically of a similar age and developmental level and do not demonstrate sexual obsession during this play. Because public sexual play is usually socially unacceptable, children may feel embarrassed or guilty if they are caught, and are likely to stop engaging in sexual play once they have been reprimanded (Briggs 2012; Staiger 2005). Harmful sexual behaviour tends to be age inappropriate, persistent, and aggressive, and involving a power imbalance between participants (Briggs 2012).

Children's displays of sexual behaviour: attitudes and influences

The notions of childhood purity, vulnerability, and innocence as dominant Western views have meant that children who step out of these bounds may be viewed as evil, corrupted, or, at minimum, a threat to social order (Barter & Berridge 2011; Staiger 2005). Barter and Berridge (2011) and Staiger (2005) argue that responses and attitudes vary towards children whose behaviour challenges social norms. Barter and Berridge (2011) suggest that socially undesirable behaviour often results in moral panic, intervention, policy change, punishment, or criminal charges. Children may thus be labelled, isolated, or marginalised. Staiger (2005) adds that some adults deny or minimise the behaviour, whilst others are outraged and condemn the child. Many of these responses are unhelpful to the child who exhibits such behaviour. The continuation of the 'victim' mindset and the notion of protecting them often leaves the child who initiated the behaviour vulnerable to being labelled as a 'perpetrator', 'offender', or 'abuser' (Bonner, Walker, & Berliner 1999). When we think in terms of 'victim' and 'perpetrator', we are unconsciously categorising children as good and innocent, or bad and evil. This is likely to affect how we respond to children.

There is a range of stimuli or influences that can make children vulnerable to engaging in harmful sexual behaviour and characteristics that have been evidenced to increase children's risk. These include child characteristics, familial influences, and their social context. We cover this in detail in Chapter 5. For this introduction, we concentrate on cultural change and the rise of social issues that are evidenced to be associated with children's sexual display.

Firstly, there has been a rise in sexual signifiers and pornography access in Western societies, which has contributed to an increase in sexualised display in general media. Many scholars argue that sexual signifiers are omnipresent and that there has been an increase in the frequency and intensity of sexualised media over the past decade, in parallel with the growth of the pornography industry. Such media dominate public spaces with sexualised images and messages that are impossible to avoid (Andsager & Roe 2003; Buckingham, Willett, Bragg, & Russell 2010; Burke, Gridley, & Pham 2008; Casciani 2010; Flood 2009; Levin & Kilbourne 2008; Papadopoulos 2010; Rush & La Nauze 2006a, 2006b; Silmalis 2010; Villani 2001; Zurbriggen et al. 2007). Analyses of Western cultural semiotics have identified a movement of sex-industry iconography into mainstream society. Examples include celebrities in revealing poses in magazines; barely clad sport celebrities and firemen in specialised calendars; the rise of pole dancing as an exercise regime; the normalisation of Brazilian waxing as standard for personal grooming; and a greater presence of pornographic signifiers in media (Attwood 2009; Ey & McInnes 2015; Holland & Attwood 2009; Walter 2010). In conjunction with these trends, dynamic developments in 'information and communication technologies have allowed new forms of pornography production and exchange' (Flood 2009, p. 385), including unlimited access regardless of one's age (Australian Communications and Media Authority 2007; Gutnick, Robb, Takeuchi, & Kotler 2011; Hennessy 2010; Linn 2012). According to the American Psychology Association Taskforce, '12% of all Web sites are pornography sites' (Zurbriggen et al. 2007, p. 10). This has resulted in a significant number of children accessing or being exposed to pornography on the internet, either accidently or deliberately (Flood 2009). According to Flood (2009), multiple studies have shown that exposure to pornography shapes adolescents' and young people's sexual experiences. They attempt to re-enact aggressive sexual acts they have viewed in pornography, and in turn act in sexually aggressive ways (Wright, Tokunaga, & Kraus 2016). This is not surprising, since observational learning is a key process in children's acquisition of cultural knowledge (Richert, Robb, & Smith 2011). The behaviours to which children are exposed become part of their cognitive and behavioural repertoire (Hall, West, & Hill 2011; Sanson et al. 2000; Timmerman et al. 2008). Therefore, if children are exposed to pornography, either accidently or deliberately, it is likely some will imitate the behaviours they see. This can involve harmful sexual behaviour.

Another key social concern is the steady rise in child sexual abuse. In Australia, on average, child sexual abuse has risen 6% for children aged 0–14 years, between 2011 and 2014 (Australian Bureau of Statistics 2017–18). According to the Australian Institute of Family Studies (2017a), there were 5,559 substantiated cases of sexual abuse towards

6 Introduction

Table 1.1 Number of substantiated cases of sexual abuse towards children during 2015–16

NSW	VIC	QLD	WA	SA	TAS	ACT	NT
2,868	1,463	267	696	152	35	24	54

children during 2015–16. This accounted for 12.2% of abuse cases. These are broken out by state and territory (Table 1.1). A range of Australian studies (n = 5) conducted between 2007 and 2015 sought adults' reports of childhood occurrences of sexual abuse. The studies found that 1.4% to 7.5% of males reported penetrative sexual abuse and 5.2% to 12% reported non-penetrative abuse, whilst 4% to 12% of females reported experiences of penetrative abuse and 14% to 26.8% reported non-penetrative abuse (Australian Institute of Family Studies 2017b). Briggs (2012) observes that it is difficult to measure the number of child abuse victims as many children do not disclose. A great deal of research correlates sexual abuse of young children with harmful sexual behaviour (Baker et al. 2008; Baker, Schneiderman, & Parker 2001; Johnson 1988, 1989; Shaw, Lewis, Loeb, Rosado, & Rodriguez 2000; Silovsky & Niec 2002; Sperry & Gilbert 2005). If child sexual abuse continues to increase, so will children's harmful sexual behaviour.

Overview of the chapters

Chapter 2 builds on the argument laid out in the introduction, about children as sexual beings, and provides more depth in relation to children's natural sexual development. We review how typical sexual development is displayed in children's behaviour and discuss how children are culturally socialised in sexual expression and suppression. We then explore definitions of harmful sexual behaviour, highlighting the diversity in language and labels before identifying and discussing children's displays of concerning and harmful sexual behaviour. Chapter 2 concludes by advocating the need for consistency in terminology and defining children's sexual behaviours.

Chapter 3 discusses what is known about the prevalence of harmful sexual behaviour in young children and pre-adolescents, drawing on international scholarly research across multiple disciplines. Much of the published material has explored children living in out-of-home care or those receiving treatment for harmful sexual behaviour, rather than those in education settings. The chapter then draws on research specific to Australia across disciplines and contexts before presenting research on the types

Introduction 7

of harmful sexual behaviour reported in education settings. This chapter concludes with a discussion of the limitations of the presented studies, identifying the gaps in current knowledge and providing recommendations for further research.

Chapter 4 draws on collective scholarly research to explore some of the social, psychological, physical, and cognitive implications for children who display harmful sexual behaviour and examines how these manifest into damaging and complex life-long harms. There are many effects of harmful sexual behaviour; these first four chapters set the scene for some of the problems associated with the issue.

There is no single explanation for what causes the development of harmful sexual behaviour. However, there are characteristics and circumstances that heighten children's vulnerabilities. Chapter 5 reviews scholarly literature regarding children's individual characteristics that make them vulnerable to both sexual exploitation and harmful sexual behaviour. For example, research demonstrates a correlation between some children who have been sexually abused and their displays of harmful sexual behaviour. Additionally, children who display harmful sexual behaviour are more likely to attract the attention of potential abusers. In particular, young children who have been sexually abused have yet to develop the cognitive ability to understand appropriate sexual expression. The chapter also examines aspects of children's social environments that have been evidenced as increasing children's vulnerability to developing harmful sexual behaviours, providing insight into influencing factors for educators and other professionals whose work involves supporting children's wellbeing.

There is a fine line between harmful sexual behaviour and sexual crime. Chapter 6 examines harmful sexual behaviour through an Australian legal lens, providing a critical assessment of the ways in which the family law system intersects with child protection issues. It discusses the complexities that arise when harmful sexual behaviour is grounded in abuse within families. It explains state and federal legislation relating to sexual behaviour in children under the age of 18 years and illustrates how Australian legislation has informed school policy and practice. It establishes the legal responsibility for Australian education departments, educators, and other professionals to uphold their duty of care to children.

Chapter 7 builds on Chapters 2 and 5 by presenting findings from a small-scale national Australian study that explored preschool, primary school, and after-school-hours care educators' understanding of typical and harmful sexual behaviour. Current training for educators specific to children's harmful sexual behaviour is hard to establish because there are no known stand-alone training modules for educators in Australia. Chapter 7 reviews current state and territory guidelines alongside a research-informed understanding of the supports educators would like in order to supportively manage children's harmful sexual behaviour. This chapter concludes by proposing a move towards a national approach.

The responses of education departments to children involved in harmful sexual behaviour in education settings vary by state and territory, and these responses depend on the legislation of the relevant state or territory, as well as school policy. Chapter 8 discusses recommended practice through a sociological lens, whilst drawing on current practices and guidelines designed to protect and support the children involved. The final focus of this chapter is on supporting children within an educational context, placing the child and their education and development at the forefront, rather than focusing only on the behaviour. Some practical ideas are deliberated.

Drawing on Bronfenbrenner's Bio-Ecological Systems Theory, Chapter 9 explores the multitude of influences on children's harmful sexual behaviour, from children's individual characteristics through to their social and legal contexts. It discusses how these interconnect to work with or against the child. Current challenges in preventative strategies are highlighted; in particular, sexualised media and access to unmonitored technologies are discussed. Keeping with the education theme of the book, recommendations in preventative strategies are presented.

The conclusion (Chapter 10) draws together the key learnings from this persistent social issue. These learnings carry grave implications if we fail to collectively reduce and manage the incidence of harmful sexual behaviour in education sites and wider society. The need for protection from exposure to influences such as pornography is likely to remain a continuing challenge, as is the need for professionals who can recognise and respond effectively to the needs of children and their families.

References

Andsager, J & Roe, K 2003, '"What's your definition of dirty, baby?": Sex in music video', *Sexuality and Culture*, vol. 7, no. 3, pp. 79–97.
Archard, D 1993, *Children: Rights & childhood*, Routledge, London.
Attwood, F 2009, 'Introduction', in F Attwood (ed), *Mainstreaming sex: The sexualisation of Western culture*, I.B. Tauris, London.
Australian Bureau of Statistics 2017–18, *Recorded crime: Victims, Australia*, Australian Bureau of Statistics, Canberra, <www.abs.gov.au/AUSSTATS/abs@.nsf/Lookup/4519.0Main+Features12017-18?OpenDocument>.
Australian Communications and Media Authority 2007, *Media and communications in Australian families 2007: Report of the media and society research project*, Commonwealth of Australia, Melbourne, viewed December 2007,

Australian Institute of Family Studies 2017a, *The prevalence of child abuse and neglect*, Australian Institute of Family Studies, Melbourne, Victoria, <https://aifs.gov.au/cfca/publications/prevalence-child-abuse-and-neglect>.

Australian Institute of Family Studies 2017b, *Child abuse and neglect statistics*, Australian Institute of Family Studies, Canberra, viewed 15 March, <https://aifs.gov.au/cfca/publications/child-abuse-and-neglect-statistics>.

Baker, AJL, Gries, L, Schneiderman, M, Parker, R, Archer, M & Friedrich, B 2008, 'Children with problematic sexualised behaviours in the child welfare system', *Child Welfare*, vol. 87, no. 1, pp. 5–27.

Baker, AJL, Schneiderman, M & Parker, R 2001, 'A survey of problematic sexualized behaviors of children in the New York City child welfare system: Estimates of problem, impact on services, and need for training', *Journal of Child Sexual Abuse*, vol. 10, no. 4, pp. 67–80.

Barter, C & Berridge, D 2011, 'Introduction', in CBD Berridge (ed), *Children behaving badly? Peer violence between children and young people*, John Wiley & Sons Ltd., Chichester, UK, pp. 1–18.

Bonner, BL, Walker, CE & Berliner, L 1999, *Children with sexual behavior problems: Assessment and treatment*, U.S Department of Health and Human Service.

Briggs, F 2012, *Child protection: The essential guide for teachers and other professionals whose work involves children*, Jo-Jo Publishing, Docklands, Victoria.

Buckingham, D, Willett, R, Bragg, S & Russell, R 2010, *External research on sexualised goods aimed at children*, The Scottish Parliament – Equal Opportunities Committee, Scotland, <www.scottish.parliament.uk/s3/committees/equal/reports-10/eor10-02.htm>.

Bullough, VL 2004, 'Children and adolescents as sexual being: A historical overview', *Child and Adolescent Psychiatric Clinics*, vol. 13, no. 3, pp. 447–459.

Burke, S, Gridley, H & Pham, H 2008, *Submission to the inquiry into the sexualisation of children in contemporary media*, The Australian Psychological Society Ltd, Melbourne, viewed April 2008, <www.psychology.org.au>.

Casciani, D 2010, 'Young "exposed to sexual imagery"', viewed 1 March 2010, <http://newsvote.bbc.co.uk/mpapps/pagetools/print/news.bbc.co.uk/2/hi/uk_news/85377>.

Cunningham, H 2005, *Children and childhood in Western society since 1500*, 2nd edn, Pearson Education Limited, Harlow.

Darian-Smith, K 2010, 'Children', *Sydney Journal*, vol. 2, no. 2, pp. 1–9.

DeLamater, J & Friedrich, WN 2002, 'Human sexual development', *The Journal of Sex Research*, vol. 39, no. 1, pp. 10–14.

Ey, L & McInnes, E 2015, 'Sexualised music videos broadcast on Australian free-to-air television in child friendly time-periods', *Children Australia*, vol. 40, no. 1, pp. 58–68.

Flood, M 2009, 'The harms of pornography exposure among children and young people', *Child Abuse Review*, vol. 18, pp. 384–400.

Freud, S 2014, *On sexual theories of children*, Read Books Ltd, Worcestershire, UK.

Gutnick, AL, Robb, MB, Takeuchi, L & Kotler, J 2011, *Always connected: The new digital media habits of young children*, The Joan Ganz Cooney Center at Sesame Workshop, New York.

Hall, PC, West, JH & Hill, S 2011, 'Sexualisation in lyrics of popular music from 1959 to 2009: Implications for sexuality educators', *Sexuality and Culture*, vol. 16, pp. 103–117, viewed 5 September 2011, <https://doi.org/10.1007/s12119-011-9103-4>, <www.springerlink.com/content/u777062808r5j228/>.

Hennessy, C 2010, 'Warning: Media can be hazardous to youth's health', viewed 28 April 2010, <www.newstimes.com/health/article/Warning-Media-can-be-hazardous-to-youths-health>.

Holland, S & Attwood, F 2009, 'Keeping fit in six inch heels: The mainstreaming of pole dancing', in F Attwood (ed), *Mainstreaming sex: The sexualisation of Western culture*, I.B. Tauris, London, pp. 165–181.

Johnson, TC 1988, 'Child perpetrators – children who molest other children: Preliminary findings', *Child Abuse & Neglect*, vol. 12, no. 2, pp. 219–229.

Johnson, TC 1989, 'Female child perpetrators: Children who molest other children', *Child Abuse & Neglect*, vol. 13, no. 4, pp. 571–585.

Levin, D & Kilbourne, J 2008, *So sexy so soon: The new sexualized childhood and what parents can do to protect their kids*, Ballantine Books, New York.

Linn, S 2012, *Healthy kids in a digital world: A strategic plan to reduce screen time for children 0–5 through organizational policy and practice change*, <http://commercialfreechildhood.org/sites/default/files/Healthy%20Kids%20in%20a%20Digital%20World.pdf>.

Papadopoulos, L 2010, *Sexualisation of young people: Review*, Home Office Publication, London.

Parke, R & Gauvain, M 2009, *Child psychology: A contemporary viewpoint*, 7th edn, McGraw-Hill, Boston.

Richert, RA, Robb, MB & Smith, EI 2011, 'Media as social partners: The social nature of young children's learning from screen media', *Child Development*, vol. 82, no. 1, pp. 82–95.

Rush, E & La Nauze, A 2006a, *Corporate paedophilia: Sexualisation of children in Australia*, The Australia Institute, Canberra, ACT, <www.tai.org.au/sites/default/files/DP90_8.pdf>.

Rush, E & La Nauze, A 2006b, *Letting children be children: Stopping the sexualisation of children in Australia*, The Australia Institute, Canberra, ACT, <www.tai.org.au/sites/default/files/DP93_8.pdf>.

Sanson, A, Duck, J, Cupit, G, Ungerer, J, Scuderi, C & Sutton, J 2000, *Media representations and responsibilities: Psychological perspectives*, The Australian Psychological Society, Melbourne, <https://pdfs.semanticscholar.org/03c2/ee6e61719869117627900e91def8b1992aff.pdf>.

Shaw, JA, Lewis, JE, Loeb, A, Rosado, J & Rodriguez, RA 2000, 'Child on child sexual abuse: Psychological perspectives', *Child Abuse & Neglect*, vol. 24, no. 12, pp. 1591–1600.

Silmalis, L 2010, 'MP slams Lady Gaga in bizarre, sexually explicit speech to parliament', *The Sunday Telegraph*, 20 March, <www.dailytelegraph.com.au/news/mp-slams-lady-gaga-in-bizarre-sexually-explicit-speech-to-parliament>.

Silovsky, J & Niec, L 2002, 'Characteristics of young children with sexual behaviour problems: A pilot study', *Child Maltreatment*, vol. 7, no. 3, pp. 187–197.

Slee, P & Schute, R 2003, *Child development: Thinking about theories*, Arnold, London.

Sperry, DM & Gilbert, BO 2005, 'Child peer sexual abuse: Preliminary data on outcomes and disclosure experiences', *Child Abuse & Neglect*, vol. 29, no. 8, pp. 889–904.

Staiger, P 2005, *Children who engage in problem sexual behaviours: Context, characteristics and treatment: A review of the literature*, Australian Childhood Foundation and Deakin University, Melbourne.

Swain, S, Warne, E & Hillel, M 2004, 'Ignorance is not innocence: Sex education in Australia, 1890–1939', in C Nelson & MH Martin (eds), *Sexual pedagogies: Sex education in Britain, Australia, and America, 1879–2000*, Palgrave Macmillan, Gordonsville, pp. 33–52.

Timmerman, L, Allen, M, Jorgensen, J, Herrett-Skjellum, J, Kramer, MR & Ryan, DJ 2008, 'A review and meta-analysis examining the relationship of music content with sex, race, priming, and attitudes', *Communication Quarterly*, vol. 56, no. 3, pp. 303–324.

Villani, S 2001, 'Impact of media on children and adolescents: A 10-year review of the research', *Journal of the American Academy of Child and Adolescent Psychiatry*, vol. 40, no. 4, pp. 392–401.

Walter, N 2010, *Living dolls: The return of sexism*, Virago, London.

Worthman, CM, Plotsky, PM, Schechter, DS & Cummings, CA (eds) 2010, *Formative experiences: The interaction of caregiving, culture, and developmental psychology*, Cambridge University Press, New York.

Wright, PJ, Tokunaga, R & Kraus, A 2016, 'A meta-analysis of pornography consumption and actual acts of sexual aggression in general population studies', *Journal of Communication*, vol. 66, no. 1, pp. 183–205.

Zurbriggen, EL, Collins, RL, Lamb, S, Roberts, T, Tolman, DL, Ward, LM & Blake, J 2007, *Report of the APA task force on the sexualization of girls*, American Psychological Association, Washington, DC.

2 Typical sexual development and harmful sexual behaviour

Introduction

Supporting children's sexual development and wellbeing depends on two factors. First is that educators understand that children's sexual development begins from infancy, and the second is their knowledge of typical, concerning, and harmful sexual behaviours. Whilst our knowledge in relation to children's sexual development and sexual displays is constantly expanding, some professionals may carry reservations about children displaying any form of sexual behaviour. Such reservations may be derived from historical social constructs of children as innocent and non-sexual, whereas others may have been informed by family or spiritual values. Equally, harmful sexual behaviours must be identified and managed to support children's safety and reduce harm. It is essential that educators are able to recognise their personal, preconceived notions about childhood sexual development and express a scholarly, informed response in this space.

Many scholars have developed guidelines around typical, concerning, and harmful sexual behaviours; however, because sexual development and expression are profoundly influenced by cultural, societal, and familial values, there is no universal agreement on what is typical and what is problematic. This chapter aims to define and describe typical, concerning, and harmful sexual behaviour from a Western perspective.

Some of the language used when describing harmful sexual behaviour positions children as criminals. This language could include terms such as 'offenders', 'perpetrators', and 'abusers' (O'Brien 2010; Royal Commission into Institutional Responses to Child Sexual Abuse 2017). This book aims to shift this thinking and place the focus on the behaviour, rather than the child. If educators are not well informed about how to recognise and respond to children's sexual behaviour, they may inaccurately label children using criminal terminology, further placing children at risk

Typical sexual development 13

of isolation and psychological damage. Every educator brings personal and professional values, skills, and knowledge to professional practice that influence how each interprets and responds to harmful sexual behaviour. It is therefore important that educators are informed about children's sexual development and expression to support children's holistic development.

It is widely accepted amongst child development professionals that sexual development begins in infancy (Levin & Kilbourne 2008). Although psychosexual behaviours may not be physically distinct until adolescence, they are evident from an early age (Friedrich, Grambsch, Broughton, Kuiper, & Beilke 1991). This chapter begins by discussing how children's sexual development unfolds and how it is expressed.

Children's typical sexual development

Social influences and sexual expression

Levin and Kilbourne (2008) report that from infancy, children explore their bodies and construct knowledge about their body parts and how they function. Through such exploration, they fondle their genitals and self-stimulate (Larsson & Svedin 2001; Mesman, Harper, Edge, Bradndt, & Pemberton 2019). Male infants are capable of experiencing an erection (DeLamater & Friedrich 2002; Mesman et al. 2019). Infants' involvement in parent/child relationships means that they experience bidirectional affection, such as being nursed, hugged, or cuddled, which plays a considerable role in children's early socio-sexual and emotional development, influencing childhood relationships and other relationships later in life.

Between the ages of 1 and 2 years, children 'learn their sex (male or female) and which one applies to them' (Levin & Kilbourne 2008, p. 54). Children construct their knowledge of gender, sex, and sexuality through many different processes, including socialisation, their general experiences, their environment, interactions with families, peers, and siblings, as well as through cultural influences such as the media and the toys they play with (Levin & Kilbourne 2008). From birth, most boys and girls are treated differently. They are expected to engage in culturally valued masculine or feminine gender roles. For example, each sex is encouraged to participate in gender stereotypical play (Peterson 2010). Sexual development is thus expressed through gender roles and identities. Children, therefore, draw on their environment to develop their ideas about gender roles, sexual identity, and relationships (Simon & Gagnon 1998; Staiger 2005), a process that is commonly referred to as *social scripting* (Simon & Gagnon 1998). Simon and Gagnon propose that young children's sexual expression is not a biological necessity but is rather the initial characteristics of social

14 *Typical sexual development*

sexual learning. For example, in some cultures girls are taught to keep their knees together when wearing skirts as an early performance of learning gender roles or sexual identity, which is far removed from actual sexual experience (Simon & Gagnon 1998). By the age of 3 years, children have largely formed their gender identity (maleness or femaleness) and embrace the roles males and females are expected to perform within their culture (DeLamater & Friedrich 2002).

In preschool, children learn about the concept of marriage and will engage in 'playing house' as a means to perform and practice adult gender roles (DeLamater & Friedrich 2002; Staiger 2005). At the same time children are gaining an understanding 'that different sexual characteristics also include physical differences' (Ey, McInnes, & Rigney 2017, p. 2). As part of their natural and healthy sexual development they show an interest in other children's genitals, which may be expressed by 'playing doctor', where children engage in looking at or touching other children's sexual body parts. This is enacted in a curious and playful way, rather than to stimulate sexual arousal (Briggs 2012; DeLamater & Friedrich 2002; Mesman et al. 2019; Staiger 2005). Exhibitionism and voyeurism behaviours are also understood as typical sexual behaviours in this age group (Briggs 2012; Friedrich et al. 1991), and children may show an interest in others' bathroom activities (Briggs 2012; Staiger 2005). It is important to note, however, that natural and healthy sexual play involves non-penetrative mutual involvement between children of a similar age and stage of development (Hackett 2011; Staiger 2005).

Between 6 and 10 years of age, children's overt sexual behaviours decline (Friedrich et al. 1991). Despite this being the age at which their hormonal sexual development begins (Worthman, Plotsky, Schechter, & Cummings 2010), they are socialised to restrain from displaying any form of sexual behaviour in public (Friedrich et al. 1991; Mesman et al. 2019). Thus, they may continue to self-stimulate their own genitals and compare their genitals with same-sex peers, but such behaviour is expressed in private to conform to societal expectations (Friedrich et al. 1991; Mesman et al. 2019; Staiger 2005). At the higher end of this age group, children may engage in discussions about sex and reproduction, use scatological language and tell dirty jokes, or try to look at pictures of nude people (Briggs 2012; Mesman et al. 2019; Staiger 2005).

In direct opposition to Freud, who claims children aged 6–11 years enter a latency stage in which sexual instincts diminish (Berk 2012), Worthman et al. (2010) and Mesman et al. (2019) argue that sexual attraction begins in middle childhood, reaching subjective awareness at around the age of 10 years. Worthman et al.'s (2010) research into studies with gay-identified males and lesbians, conducted by investigators from different disciplines

Typical sexual development 15

and in different nations, found that the onset of first attraction to the same sex was at age 10. Researchers claim that there are clear psycho-behavioural trends at ages 9–10 that ignite sexual attraction, such as children reaching a new way of thinking about their bodies, gender roles, and sexual feelings. It is common for children aged 10–12 years to develop crushes (Mesman et al. 2019; Worthman et al. 2010) which are expressed through affectionate acts, such as closed mouth-kissing, holding hands, and sexual innuendo/flirting (Briggs 2012).

Physiological sexual development

Research suggests that puberty encompasses two separate maturational processes. Adrenarche (primary and hormonal) starts as early as age 6–8 (Worthman et al. 2010). Primary sexual development involves changes to the reproductive organs, ovaries, vulva, uterus, vagina, penis, scrotum, and testes, directly as a result of the release of hormones (Berk 2012). Secondary sexual development is very diverse amongst individuals, so a starting date is hard to distinguish; however, it is typically fully developed between the ages of 15–17 (Worthman et al. 2010). Secondary sexual characteristics are the visible characteristics not specifically related to the reproduction system, such as the development of pubic, underarm, and facial hair; breasts; widened hips; and the Adam's apple (Berk 2012). In conjunction with the maturation of the sex organs, there are increased levels of adrenal androgens, which reach their full peak between 10 and 12 years. Despite the underlying hormonal processes, sexual expressions depend greatly on environmental variables, including social and cultural factors (Hoffnung, Hoffnung, Seifert, Burton Smith, & Hine 2010). Because of strict controls over sexual research with children under the age of 18 years, empirical data on children's sexual engagement are scarce (Worthman et al. 2010). However, it is considered typical sexual development for adolescents to feel sexual arousal, masturbate, and engage in consensual sexual intercourse and oral sex (Briggs 2012).

Girls begin physical sexual maturation between 10 and 12 years. At this age, girls undergo a height spurt and experience hormonal changes that stimulate reproductive organ growth. Their breasts start to bud, pubic hair appears, menarche occurs, and the buttocks, hips, and thighs begin to expand. By 15 years of age, most girls have reached their adult height, and their breasts and pubic hair growth is complete (Berk 2012, 2013; Hoffnung et al. 2010; Peterson 2010; Worthman et al. 2010).

Regarding boys, Hamilton notes that 'years before a boy sees physical changes in his body, his brain releases the hormone gonadotropin, which triggers puberty' (Hamilton 2010, p. 73). Boys begin the physical

16 *Typical sexual development*

maturation process between 9.5 years and 13 years, when their testes begin to enlarge. At around age 12, they grow pubic hair and their penis enlarges, and a height spurt begins approximately six months later. They experience spermarche, and at approximately 14 years they have another height spurt and put on weight, their voice deepens, and facial hair begins to grow. At about 15 years, their penis, testes, and pubic hair growth is complete, and they have reached the peak of their strength and adult height (Berk 2012, 2013; Hoffnung et al. 2010; Peterson 2010; Worthman et al. 2010). A chorus of researchers agree that over recent decades, girls and boys are physically maturing earlier and that the age of onset of puberty is decreasing by about four months per generation (Berk 2012, 2013; Carr-Greg 2010; Hoffnung et al. 2010; Levin & Kilbourne 2008; Linn 2009; Peterson 2010; Steingraber 2009; Worthman et al. 2010).

Given the foregoing discussion, there is clearly considerable research establishing that sexual development begins from infancy and unfolds throughout the developmental process. There is also evidence that children's displays of sexual expression are grounded in social and cultural values that change over time. Because of these influences, there is no universal agreement on normative sexual behaviour. There are, however, some key characteristics that define normative sexual expression. Natural and healthy sexual expression should reflect the child's or young person's age and level of development, be mutually congenial and consensual with peers of approximately the same age, and reflect socially acceptable behaviours (Hackett 2011; Staiger 2005). The frequency of engagement in sexual displays should be generally sporadic and balanced with other aspects in life (Staiger 2005). If sexual behaviour becomes obsessive, non-consensual, or aggressive, there is a need to be concerned about the child's or young person's healthy sexual development.

Defining harmful sexual behaviour: exploring the language

There are always sensitivities when discussing harmful sexual behaviour in relation to children. It is particularly important to use clear definitions when implementing and discussing the language used to describe the behaviour. Some authors may use terms such as 'child-on-child sexual abuse', 'sexually offending behaviour', 'sexual assault', or 'sexually abusive behaviour' interchangeably with 'harmful sexual behaviour'. Such language positions children as sexual perpetrators, molesters, or offenders, establishing a label for children as criminals (Bonner, Walker, & Berliner 1999; Chaffin et al. 2008; Flanagan 2010). Such terms are grounded in a knowledge of socio-legal norms which does not reflect children's context.

Typical sexual development 17

Terms such as 'problem', 'problematic', or 'harmful' when discussing sexual behaviour are much more appropriate because they focus on the behaviour and not the child and appear to be more widely adopted in recent research. Hackett (2011) points out that the way professionals define the behaviour will influence how they respond. He argues that sexual behaviour can be seen as a continuum from normal through to violent and presents several categories of behaviour: normal, inappropriate, problematic, abusive, and violent. Hackett (2011) suggests that only the latter three categories give cause for concern. The Royal Commission into Institutional Responses to Child Sexual Abuse (2017) uses the term 'children with harmful sexual behaviours' to reflect the breadth of behaviours and complexity of issues. They argue that:

> This term covers children who display the full spectrum of sexual behaviour problems, including behaviours that are problematic to the child's own development, as well as those that are coercive, sexually aggressive and predatory towards others. Our use of the term, therefore, captures all child sexual abuse by children, including juvenile sexual offending.
> (The Royal Commission into Institutional Responses to Child Sexual Abuse 2017, p. 32)

In an education context, many child protection training resources refer to sexual behaviour as 'age appropriate', 'concerning', or 'serious' in nature (see Department for Education 2019; True Relationships & Reproductive Health 2016). Self-focused sexual behaviour, such as masturbation or genital display, can be concerning or problematic but may be more readily accepted as typical sexual development since it does not place others at risk. Intrusive sexual behaviours comprise a subset of harmful sexual behaviours that are defined as invasive and/or aggressive, involving physical contact such as touching or penetrating another's private parts (Smith, Lindsey, Bohora, & Silovsky 2019).

Children's displays of sexual behaviour need to be interpreted according to the child's developmental stage. For example, sexual behaviour that may be considered normal in young children may be considered concerning or problematic in primary or adolescent children and vice versa (Hackett 2011; Mesman et al. 2019). Harmful sexual behaviour is generally not established as a medical or psychological disorder but rather identified as a 'set of behaviours that fall well outside acceptable societal limits' (Chaffin et al. 2008, p. 3). Intrapersonal sexual behaviour, although seen as problematic, usually refers to self-directed behaviours such as public or persistent masturbation or an overt interest in sex and sexual play

(Silovsky & Niec 2002). Interpersonal harmful sexual behaviour, on the other hand, commonly refers to sexual behaviour towards peers and can be described as children imposing sexual acts on others of the same or similar age (Silovsky & Niec 2002). If there is a significant age difference, power differentials, or violence involved, then there is an element of victimisation, and this may be considered sexually abusive behaviour (Hackett 2011; Mesman et al. 2019). Children who instigate sexual acts often try to lure, threaten, persuade, trick, or bribe other children to engage in sexual activity and will generally try to conceal the behaviour from adults (Briggs 2012). It is the children that engage in these behaviours who are at greater risk of being labelled perpetrators, molesters, or offenders against other children. It is important to note that some forms of peer-on-peer harmful sexual behaviour may not include ill-intention (Flanagan 2010) or an element of victimisation. Nevertheless, such behaviour may still result in development impediments, distress, or harm to the children involved (Hackett 2011).

Assessing concerning or problematic behaviours is thus related to the frequency of the behaviour, the degree of intrusion on others, the degree of coercion involved, and aspects of visibility or secrecy.

For pre-adolescent children, harmful sexual behaviours can include:

- persistent public masturbation;
- persistent flashing of genitals, breasts, or bottoms to peers;
- having sexual knowledge above what is typically known for their age, including demonstrations or re-enactments of sexual activity, using sexual language, and teaching or sharing this with their peers;
- having an obsession with sex or an interest in pornography and sharing this with peers;
- trying to touch peers in a sexual way, including touching genitals, bottoms, or breasts, or inviting peers to touch them in these areas;
- trying to insert objects into peers' genitals, bottoms, or mouths;
- trying to put their genitals in their peers' mouths or asking peers to mouth their genitals;
- encouraging peers to engage in sexual activity whilst they watch;
- simulated or attempted intercourse;
- behaviour involving injury to self or others;
- using threats to coerce others;
- sending sexually explicit photos of self or others, or sexually explicit messages to peers;
- violating personal space or sexually harassing peers.

(Briggs 2012; El-Murr 2017; Evertsz & Miller 2012; Mesman et al. 2019; Staiger 2005)

Typical sexual development 19

For adolescents aged 13+ years, harmful sexual behaviours can also include:

- non-consensual fondling or touching of peers' genitals, breasts, or bottoms, or forcing peers to fondle or touch them in these areas, including the use of coercion, trickery, or bribery;
- non-consensual oral sex or forcing peers to perform oral sex on them;
- sending sexually explicit photos of self or others, or sexual threats to peers;
- violating personal space or sexually harassing peers;
- sexual contact with animals;
- sexual contact and/or coercion of younger children;
- stalking or being excessively persistent after being warned or rejected by peers.

(Briggs 2012; El-Murr 2017; Staiger 2005)

The potential for harm escalates when the behaviours just described are persistent or obsessive, or carry elements of aggression, or are targeted towards younger children. Children often rehearse or try out behaviours they have been exposed to as an exploration and growth strategy. If harmful sexual behaviour by a child has become a continuing issue, or if age-inappropriate sexual play has become coercive and secretive, there is an urgent protective need to intervene to support the safety of all children involved.

Peer-on-peer harmful sexual behaviour often occurs in isolated and concealed areas such as toilets, amongst heavy foliage, or behind buildings. Once detected, it is important that adults not only report the behaviour, but also support the child who engages in sexual behaviour and the other child or children involved. Strategies addressing the aftermath of harmful sexual behaviours are detailed in Chapter 4. Harmful sexual behaviours are often learned, and it is important to act quickly to prevent a cumulative effect amongst a group of children such as a class cohort at school. It is equally important to explore 'where has the child learnt this' to facilitate support services.

Conclusion

Although there is an adequate consensus amongst Western scholars about what behaviours are considered typical and problematic sexual expression across age groups, there are still some inconsistencies in the literature around terminology. It is important that educators and other professionals concerned with the wellbeing of children are aware of the discrepancies in the language used to describe children's harmful sexual behaviour in order to label the behaviour rather than the child. It is equally important that professionals have a sound understanding of the research, ideas, and conceptual frameworks to enable them to identify concerning and harmful sexual behaviour, free from the potential bias of their own values and perspectives, which may influence their interpretation of harmful sexual behaviour. This is to avoid the risk of children's normal sexual development being treated as problematic, or harmful sexual behaviours being dismissed as normal developmental behaviour. This chapter has outlined a Westernised view of these behaviours, based on the social, legal, and cultural constructs of Westernised ideologies. However, no universal definition currently exists about what constitutes harmful sexual behaviour. This chapter has attempted to provide a guide to discerning whether children's behaviour meets the criteria for concerning or harmful sexual behaviour. The following chapter examines the prevalence of harmful sexual behaviours in Australia and elsewhere.

References

Berk, L 2012, *Infants, children, and adolescents*, 7th edn, Pearson Education, Boston.

Berk, L 2013, *Child development*, 9th edn, Pearson, Boston.

Bonner, BL, Walker, CE & Berliner, L 1999, *Children with sexual behavior problems: Assessment and treatment*, U.S Department of Health and Human Service.

Briggs, F 2012, *Child protection: The essential guide for teachers and other professionals whose work involves children*, Jo-Jo Publishing, Docklands, Victoria.

Carr-Greg, DM 2010, 'Premature sexualisation', *Bratz, Britney and bralettes seminar*, Australian Council on Children and the Media; Kids free 2B Kids.

Chaffin, M, Berliner, L, Block, R, Johnson, TC, Friedrich, WN, Louis, DG, Lyon, TD, Page, IJ, Prescott, DS & Silovsky, JF 2008, 'Report of the ATSA task force on children with sexual behaviour problems', *Child Maltreatment*, vol. 13, no. 2, pp. 199–218.

DeLamater, J & Friedrich, WN 2002, 'Human sexual development', *The Journal of Sex Research*, vol. 39, no. 1, pp. 10–14.

Department for Education 2019, *Responding to problem sexual behaviour in children and young people: Guidelines for staff in education and care settings*, 3rd edn, Government of South Australia: Department for Education, Adelaide South Australia.

El-Murr, A 2017, *Problem sexual behaviours and sexually abusive behaviours in Australian children and young people: A review of available literature*, Australian Institute of Family Studies, Melbourne, Victoria, <https://aifs.gov.au/cfca/publications/problem-sexual-behaviours-and-sexually-abusive-behaviours-australian-children>.

Evertsz, J & Miller, R 2012, *Children with problem sexual behaviours and their families: Best interests case practice model: Specialist practice resource*, Victorian Government Department of Human Services, Melbourne, <www.cpmanual.vic.gov.au/sites/default/files/Children%20problem%20sexual%20behaviours%20specialist%20practice%20resource%202012%203013%20.pdf>.

Ey, L, McInnes, E & Rigney, L 2017, 'Educators' understanding of young children's typical and problematic sexual behaviour and their training in this area', *Sex Education*, vol. 17, no. 6, pp. 682–696.

Flanagan, P 2010, 'Making molehills into mountains: Adults responses to child sexuality and behaviour', *Explorations: An E Journal of Narrative Practice*, no. 1, pp. 57–69.

Friedrich, WN, Grambsch, P, Broughton, D, Kuiper, J & Beilke, RL 1991, 'Normative sexual behaviour in children', *Pediatrics*, vol. 88, no. 3, pp. 456–464.

Hackett, S 2011, 'Children and young people with harmful sexual behaviours', in C Barter & D Berridge (eds), *Children behaving badly? Peer violence between children and young people*, John Wiley & Sons Ltd, Chichester.

Hamilton, M 2010, *What's happening to our boys?*, Penguin, Camberwell, Victoria.

Hoffnung, M, Hoffnung, RJ, Seifert, KL, Burton Smith, R & Hine, A 2010, *Childhood*, John Wiley & Sons Australia, Ltd, Milton.

Larsson, I & Svedin, C-G 2001, 'Sexual behaviour in Swedish preschool children, as observed by their parents', *Acta Paediatric*, vol. 90, no. 4, pp. 436–444.

Levin, D & Kilbourne, J 2008, *So sexy so soon: The new sexualized childhood and what parents can do to protect their kids*, Ballantine Books, New York.

Linn, S 2009, 'A royal juggernaut: The Disney princesses and other commercialized threats to creative play and the path to realisation for young girls', in S Olfman (ed), *The sexualization of childhood*, Praeger, Westport, pp. 33–50.

Mesman, GR, Harper, SL, Edge, NA, Brandt, TW & Pemberton, JL 2019, 'Problematic sexual behaviour in children', *Journal of Pediatric Health Care*, vol. 33, no. 3, pp. 323–331.

O'Brien, W 2010, *Australia's response to sexualised or sexually abuse behaviours in children and young people*, Australian Crime Commission, Canberra, ACT, <http://dro.deakin.edu.au/eserv/DU:30065114/obrien-australias-2010.pdf>.

Peterson, C 2010, *Looking forward through the lifespan: Developmental psychology*, 5th edn, Pearson Australia, Frenchs Forest.

Royal Commission into Institutional Responses to Child Sexual Abuse 2017, *Final report: Volume 10, children with harmful sexual behaviours*, Sydney, <www.childabuseroyalcommission.gov.au/sites/default/files/final_report_-_volume_10_children_with_harmful_sexual_behaviours.pdf>.

Silovsky, J & Niec, L 2002, 'Characteristics of young children with sexual behaviour problems: A pilot study', *Child Maltreatment*, vol. 7, no. 3, pp. 187–197.

Simon, W & Gagnon, J 1998, 'Psychosexual development', *Society*, vol. 35, no. 2, pp. 60–67.

Smith, TJ, Lindsey, RA, Bohora, S & Silovsky, JF 2019, 'Predictors of intrusive sexual behaviors in preschool-aged children', *The Journal of Sex Research*, vol. 56, no. 2, pp. 229–238, <https://doi.org/10.1080/00224499.2018.1447639>

Staiger, P 2005, *Children who engage in problem sexual behaviours: Context, characteristics and treatment: A review of the literature*, Australian Childhood Foundation and Deakin University, Melbourne.

Steingraber, S 2009, 'Girls gone grown up: Why are U.S. girls reaching puberty earlier and earlier?', in S Olfman (ed), *The sexualization of childhood*, Praeger, Westport, pp. 51–63.

True Relationships & Reproductive Health 2016, *Sexual behaviour in children and young people: A guide to identify, understand and respond to sexual behaviours*, True Relationships & Reproductive Health, Queensland, <www.true.org.au/Resources/shop#!/Traffic-Lights-brochure/p/57318729>.

Worthman, CM, Plotsky, PM, Schechter, DS & Cummings, CA (eds) 2010, *Formative experiences: The interaction of caregiving, culture, and developmental psychology*, Cambridge University Press, New York.

3 Children's harmful sexual behaviour

A global phenomenon?

Introduction

In the past 20 years there have been numerous state and federal Australian government inquiries into child sexual abuse and child protection that have highlighted high levels of sexual abuse of children in institutions and concerns about harmful sexual behaviours among children. These include at least 11 state government inquiries into child protection systems and their responses to maltreated children, including abuse of children living in out-of-home care (Carmody 2013; Debelle 2013; Family and Community Development Committee 2013; Forde 1999; Gordon, Hallahan, & Henry 2002; Layton 2003; Mullighan 2008; New South Wales Legislative Council 2017; Nyland 2016; O'Halloran 2011; Victoria Parliament 2013; Wild & Anderson 2007). There have also been three federal government inquiries examining experiences of children living in institutional care and children engaging with institutions such as schools, religious and welfare organisations, and sporting and recreation groups (Senate Community Affairs Reference Committee 2001, 2004; Royal Commission into Institutional Responses to Child Sexual Abuse 2017a). Similar inquiries have been conducted internationally, including Ireland (Murphy, Buckley, & Joyce 2005; Murphy, Mangan, & O'Niell 2009, 2010; Ryan 2009); the United Kingdom (Hart, Lane, & Doherty 2017); and Canada (McDonald, Des Roisers, Boniface, Owen, & Buchanan 2000). These inquiries have collectively provided much evidence that government child protection systems and community organisations have often failed to protect children and also provided alternative care environments which have exposed children to further sexual, physical, and emotional abuse. These documented widespread failures to protect children from abuse or to respond adequately in the immediate or longer term provide a backdrop to the social contexts which create risks for the development of harmful sexual behaviours.

Determining the prevalence of child maltreatment, child sexual abuse, or children engaging in harmful sexual behaviour is fraught with difficulty. This is partly due to the varying definitions of what constitutes maltreatment, abuse, or harmful sexual behaviour. Further problems are posed by inconsistencies in methodology, including data collection techniques, the type and population from which the research sample is drawn, and the number and wording of questions (Bromfield, Hirte, Octoman, & Katz 2017; Norman et al. 2012). We know that child sexual abuse is grossly under-reported (Royal Commission into Institutional Responses to Child Sexual Abuse 2017b), and this may be related to children's fear of negative consequences, not being believed or getting in trouble, embarrassment, feelings of guilt (Briggs 2012), or children not understanding consent, resulting in them not recognising that they were being sexually abused (National Society for the Prevention of Cruelty to Children 2018). It is therefore expected that incidents of harmful sexual behaviours are also under-reported.

Although there is significant debate about how to describe children and young people displaying sexualised behaviour without labelling them as sex offenders, much of the research that provides data on children's high-level harmful sexual behaviour comes from the child welfare and criminal justice systems. In Australia, this means that consistent data are only collected on children aged 10+ years who have been charged with a sexual assault crime. Lower-age groups' harmful sexual behaviour is generally not recorded through the criminal system, and there are no national or international studies that can be generalised, to the authors' knowledge. Nevertheless, there is enough research internationally and within Australia to establish that this is an issue of concern.

This chapter aims to report research on post-pubertal children's high-level harmful sexual behaviour, which often finds them criminalised, through to the types of sexual behaviour displayed by young children and pre-adolescents in education settings. It also discusses international small-scale studies that report on children's harmful sexual behaviour.

As discussed in the previous chapter, children's sexual expressions in education settings are not always problematic, particularly if they are a once-off incident. The fine line between socially unacceptable public sexual expression and behaviours of concern is highlighted. This chapter begins by presenting data on children's harmful sexual behaviour that has resulted in children being criminally charged with a sexual offence that is recorded permanently. The chapter then discusses a series of studies that have explored children's harmful sexual behaviour within particular contexts; however, these are commonly small-scale studies that can only provide a snapshot of the experiences by the participants at the time and cannot be generalised.

Prevalence of harmful sexual behaviour

Recent criminal statistics demonstrate that Australian children aged 10–18 years are increasingly being charged with sexual crimes. According to the Australian Bureau of Statistics (2017–18), 1,211 children aged 10–17 years were convicted of sexual assault and related offences between the 1 June 2017 and 30 July 2018. Of these children, 14 (1.1%) were aged 10 years, 27 (2.2%) aged 11, 74 (6.1%) aged 12, 143 (12%) aged 13, 42 (3.5%) aged 14, 254 (21%) aged 15, 247 (20.4%) aged 16, and 211 (17.4%) aged 17. These assaults accounted for approximately 15% of Australian sexual assaults recorded in 2017–18. The recent Royal Commission into Institutional Responses to Child Sexual Abuse heard more than 8,000 personal stories and more than 1,000 written accounts from survivors (Royal Commission into Institutional Responses to Child Sexual Abuse 2017a). Of those who came forward, 1,129 reported being sexually abused by another child. Of those, 473 (41.9%) said that they were abused by another child or children only, and 656 (58.1%) said that they were abused by both adults and other children. Some of these survivors also revealed that they had then sexually abused other children (Royal Commission into Institutional Responses to Child Sexual Abuse 2017c). Studies show, however, that the average recidivism rates for harmful sexual behaviours that reach a criminal threshold range from 3–14% (Royal Commission into Institutional Responses to Child Sexual Abuse 2017c).

In the United States, the most recent data for juvenile convictions related to sexual assault is reported under violent crimes, which also include murder, rape, assault, and robbery. Consequently, data specific to sexual crime is difficult to find. Data from 2010 reported sexually related crimes separately and showed that in 2010, 2,900 children under the age of 18 were convicted of forcible rape, 1,000 were convicted of prostitution, and 13,000 were convicted of other sex offences (Sickmund & Puzzanchera 2014). Data from 2012 found that 12,400 youth were charged with sex offences (not including forcible rape and prostitution), and approximately 50% of these youth were under 15 years of age (National Center for Juvenile Justice 2012). Statistics released by the Office of Juvenile Justice and Delinquency Prevention in 2017 in relation to sexual assault victims found that approximately 38% of children under the age of 6 years, 42% of children aged 6–11 years, and 31% of youth aged 12–17 years were sexually assaulted by children under the age of 18 years. Of these assaults, 27% were committed by children under the age of 12 years (Mesman, Harper, Edge, Brandt, & Pemberton 2019).

In the United Kingdom, the number of sexual offences committed by children appears to be increasing dramatically. Between 2012 and 2015 there were more than 5,500 allegations of sexual crimes in schools reported to police, 20% of which were child peer-on-peer sexual abuse (Parliament UK 2016). According to a BBC Freedom of Information request, the number of police-recorded sexual offences by under-18-year-olds against other under-18-year-olds in England and Wales rose by 71% between 2013–14 (4,603) and 2016–17 (7,866) (NSPCC 2019). The National Society for the Prevention of Cruelty to Children (NSPCC) (2018, 2019) reported that approximately one third of child sexual abuse is committed by other children and young people in the United Kingdom. The Childline service in the United Kingdom delivered 3,000 counselling sessions to children and young people who were concerned about having been sexually abused by their peers (Department for Education 2018; NSPCC 2018). The NSPCC also state that they receive many enquiries from parents and professionals who are concerned about children displaying sexualised behaviour. In 2016–17, there were 663 contacts to their helpline about this (NSPCC 2018).

Research has identified that children and young people living in residential care are at a significantly increased risk of peer sexual violence (McKibbin 2017; Moore, McArthur, Death, Tilbury, & Rochea 2017). Several studies have explored harmful sexual behaviour within out-of-home care settings. A study conducted across 48 welfare agencies offering out-of-home placement services in New York found that of the 31,103 child residents, harmful sexual behaviour was displayed by 11% of children in foster boarding homes and agency-operated boarding homes, 17% of children residing in group homes, and 30% of children in residential treatment centres (Baker, Schneiderman, & Parker 2001). Research conducted to test the Child Sexual Behavior Inventory (CSBI) was developed by Friedrich (1997) with nonparental reporters. Baker et al. (2008) interviewed foster parents and primary therapists (social workers) from three New York child welfare agencies about the prevalence of harmful sexual behaviour relative to 97 randomly selected children (aged 10–12 years) from either foster boarding homes or residential treatment centres. Results found that 34% of the children in the residential treatment centre sample and 12% of the children in the foster boarding homes sample displayed sexually abusive behaviours.

Research conducted with 194 children who had been sexually abused (51 who had been abused by another child and 143 who had been abused by an adult), enlisted from the Florida Department of Child and Family Services, found that of the 51 children who had been sexually abused by another child, 16% were abused at school (Shaw, Lewis, Loeb, Rosado, & Rodriguez 2000). Johnson (1988, 1989) investigated two groups of children who were enrolled in a Los Angeles program for children with harmful sexual behaviour. Her research with 47 boys, aged 4–13 years, reported that these boys engaged in penetrative behaviours, including vaginal, anal, and oral copulation. For 29% of these children, behaviours began when they were 4–6 years of age, 20% began at age 7–9 years, and 51% began at the age of 10–12 years. These boys engaged in these activities with children whom they knew, aged between 1–15 years (Johnson 1988). Johnson's (1989) research with 13 girls, aged 4–12 years, reported that these girls mainly engaged in non-penetrative behaviours such as fondling and genital contact. However, they also engaged in oral copulation, simulated intercourse, and vaginal and anal penetration. The age at which these girls began acting out sexually ranged between 4 and 9 years, whilst the children they acted out on were aged 1–11 years. Similar research conducted by Silovsky and Niec (2002) that surveyed caregivers of 47 children (aged 3–7 years) enrolled in a treatment program for sexual behaviour problems reported that 54% of children tried to touch other children's genitals after being told not to, 43% tried to undress other children against their will, 38% tried to have sexual intercourse, 27% tried to have oral sex, 22% tried to undress adults against their will, 19% forced other children into sexual acts, 16% put fingers or objects into other children's vaginas or rectums, and 11% planned how to sexually touch other children (Silovsky & Niec 2002, p. 193).

A more recent study by Silovsky, Niec, Bard, and Hecht (2007), with caregivers of children aged 3–7 years, referred to a program for children who display harmful sexual behaviour. It reported that 'all 85 children demonstrated interpersonal sexual behaviours (involving another person), and many had sexually aggressive behaviours' (Silovsky et al. 2007, p. 385).

These studies demonstrate that the severity and prevalence of children displaying harmful sexual behaviours warrant treatment programs for children with these behaviours in the United States. Despite the limited research on harmful sexual behaviour in Australia, the issue is clearly of similar concern given several research reviews exploring best practice to support these children over the past few years. Recent publications include 'Rapid evidence assessment: Current best evidence in the therapeutic treatment of children with problem or harmful sexual behaviours, and children who have sexually offended' (Shlonsky et al. 2017), and 'Service models for children under 10 with problematic sexual behaviours: An evidence check rapid review brokered by the Sax Institute for the NSW Ministry of Health' (Cox, Ey, Parkinson, & Bromfield 2018).

A US longitudinal study explored 8-year-old children's harmful sexual behaviour, examining the prevalence and types of children's sexual behaviour, the correlation of maltreatment, and caregivers' and teachers' ratings of emotional and behavioural concerns for children who display interpersonal harmful sexual behaviours (sexual behaviours that involve another individual). Results found that 245 (22%) of 1,112 children displayed these behaviours, including inviting others to engage in sexual activity, emulating sexual intercourse, touching others' genitals, oral sex advances, attempting to undress others against their will, and trying to fondle animals in a sexual way. Harmful sexual behaviour was correlated with child maltreatment (Allen 2016).

A longitudinal study to explore the development trajectories of children's sexual behaviours involved 354 normative Canadian children aged 3–8 years and found that more than 61% of the children aged 3–5 years and 45% of children aged 6–8 years showed at least one incident of sexually intrusive behaviour (Lussier, McCuish, Mathesius, Corrado, & Nadeau 2017). Sexually intrusive behaviour measured included: 'touches another child's sex parts; asks others to engage in sexual acts; attempts to undress others against their will; oral sex with another child; showing sexual parts to other children; touches an adult sex parts; tries to look at people in the nude/undressing; and tries to have sexual intercourse with another child' (Lussier et al. 2017, p. 632). Children fell into four developmental trajectories: very low, low declining, moderate stable, and high-rate increasing. Just over 13% of children displayed high-rate increasing sexual behaviour which is considered harmful sexual behaviour. Children who displayed high-rate increasing sexual behaviour showed a significantly higher annual frequency of sexual behaviour as early as 4 years of age. Their behaviour became more frequent and extensive with age, and they did not show the behavioural inhibitions expected for typical sexual development (Lussier et al. 2017).

A Croatian study exploring the prevalence of contact and non-contact child sexual abuse and the relationship of the perpetrators surveyed 3,175 children aged 11 years (n = 1033), 13 years (n = 1018), and 16 years (n = 1124). This nationally representative probabilistic stratified cluster sample comprised 2.62% of the overall population of children aged 11, 13, and 16 years. The study found that 10.8% of the sample had experienced some form of sexual abuse in their lifetime, and 7.7% had experienced sexual abuse within the past year (Marina Ajduković & Sušac 2013). Of the children who had experienced non-contact sexual abuse in the past year, 57.2% of the 11-year-old girls, 66.7% of the 13-year-old girls, and 58.1% of the 16-year-old girls were abused by another child. Of the girls who had experienced contact sexual abuse within the past year, 76.8% of the 11-year-olds, 78.3% of the 13-year-olds, and 57.6% of the 16-year-olds were abused by another child. For the boys, 37.7% of the 11-year-olds, 77.4% of the 13-year-olds, and 97.2% of the 16-year-olds experienced non-contact sexual abuse by another child. A total of 100% of the 11-year-olds, 96.4% of 13-year-olds, and 95% of the 16-year-olds experienced contact sexual abuse by another child (Marina Ajduković & Sušac 2013).

Children's harmful sexual behaviour 29

These studies demonstrate that children's displays of harmful sexual behaviour are prevalent across multiple countries and involve children across the age spectrum. Many of the behaviours identified and discussed are interpersonal and largely classified as abusive sexual behaviours, particularly in older children.

Prevalence of harmful sexual behaviour in Australia and the context where it occurs

In Australia, data on children with problematic or harmful sexualised behaviours are not collected uniformly, and issues such as nondisclosure, a general lack of knowledge of healthy and harmful sexual behaviour, and denial or minimisation of incidents mean that the prevalence of children displaying harmful sexual behaviours is difficult to determine (O'Brien 2010). As outlined earlier, the Royal Commission into Institutional Responses to Child Sexual Abuse (2017a) found that of those who came forward, 1,129 reported being sexual abused by another child; 498 survivors were abused by another child in a religious institution (Royal Commission into Institutional Responses to Child Sexual Abuse 2017g); 65 were abused by another child in contemporary out-of-home care (Royal Commission into Institutional Responses to Child Sexual Abuse 2017d); 14 were abused by another child in sporting, recreation, arts, culture, community, or hobby groups (Royal Commission into Institutional Responses to Child Sexual Abuse 2017f); 16 were abused by another child in a detention centre (Royal Commission into Institutional Responses to Child Sexual Abuse 2017h); and 308 were abused by another child in a school (Royal Commission into Institutional Responses to Child Sexual Abuse 2017e). Given that these statistics are calculated only from those who came forward to report their abuse and who communicated the age of the person who harmed them, it is predicted that these statistics under-represent the true numbers of children who have been sexually abused by children with harmful sexual behaviours. Other studies have shown that between 30–60% of childhood sexual abuse is enacted by children and young people (El-Murr 2017).

Dr Joe Tucci, chief executive officer of the Australian Childhood Foundation, presented evidence to the Royal Commission into Institutional Responses to Child Sexual Abuse (2016) in Out-of-Home Care. He stated that

> Victoria has introduced legislation, as part of their Child Protection Act that makes it mandatory for young people who engage in problem sexual behaviour to be diverted to a therapeutic service within the child protection context rather than to have to be prosecuted in the

justice area. When we first started our first program 15 years ago, we had about 10 referrals a year. We are now up to about 250, and that is just for two regions of the state in Victoria.

(Royal Commission into Institutional Responses to Child Sexual Abuse 2016, p. 38)

This suggests that the prevalence of harmful sexual behaviour in children is increasing.

Harmful sexual behaviour in education settings: preschools, schools, and out-of-school care

National and international research demonstrates that children and young people experience and display sexual behaviours in education settings. International research into young children's (2–6 years) sexual behaviour in educational settings shows that it is prevalent in child care centres and preschools; however, their sexual behaviour was largely typical sexual expression rather than problematic, with only a small number of children displaying behaviours that were cause for concern (Davies, Glaser, & Kossoff 2000; Larsson & Svedin 2002; Lindblad, Gustafsson, Larsson, & Lundin 1995). International research in primary schools (Gillander 2012) and high schools (Clear et al. 2014; Hill & Kearl 2011), however, has evidenced peer-to-peer sexual harassment and assault in the school context. It is unclear whether the difference between children's sexual behaviour in education settings is related to the age of the children or the age of the research.

Turner, Finkelhor, Hamby, Shattuck, and Ormrod (2011) conducted research with 2,999 children aged 0–17 years in the United States in 2008. Children who were aged 10 years or older participated in telephone interviews, and children aged under 10 years were represented by their parents, who participated in the interviews on the child's behalf. This study found that 6.6% of children had experienced peer sexual assault, rape or attempted rape, flashing, and/or sexual harassment within the previous year. Of the 243 cases reported, 1.2% of these children were aged 6–9 years, 4.9% were aged 10–13 years, 13.8% were aged 14–17 years, and 46.9% of these incidents occurred within a school or day care setting. Clear et al. (2014) conducted research with 18,090 American students in years 9–12 and found that 29.9% reported being a victim of peer sexual harassment. Of the students who reported victimisation of sexual harassment, rates were higher amongst females (37.1%) than males (21.4%). These two studies suggest that the increase in harmful sexual behaviour and sexually abusive behaviours in education settings is linked to age.

The United Kingdom 'Sexual harassment and sexual violence in schools' report states that 'data collected by the BBC in 2015 found that 5,500 sexual offences were recorded in UK schools over a three year period, including 600 rapes' (Parliament UK 2016). They further cite four large-scale survey studies that report that between 22% and 59% of young girls have been sexually harassed in a school context. Big Talk Education, an organisation that delivers education about healthy relationships and sex education, began receiving referrals regarding harmful sexual behaviour amongst students in primary schools about 12 years ago. They report that they have seen a steady increase in referrals over the years and now receive one to two referrals a week; however, they suggest that the prevalence of harmful sexual behaviour is likely to be much higher as they only work with the students that schools cannot manage within their system (Parliament UK 2016).

In Australia, the Royal Commission into Institutional Responses to Child Sexual Abuse (2017e) heard from 2,186 child sexual abuse survivors who had experienced sexual abuse in a school context. Of the survivors who disclosed the age of the person who harmed them, 14.1% reported that the person was another child. The age range of the child sexual abuse survivors varied from 18 to well over 60 years, which suggests that peer sexual assault has been prevalent in education settings for many years. A small-scale study in Australia that surveyed 107 educators working in government, independent and Catholic schools, preschools, and after-school-hours care found that 41% of educators (n = 103) reported that they had observed children displaying harmful sexual behaviour in education settings (Ey & McInnes 2018). Of the educators who reported that they had observed these behaviours, '12% reported that they had observed it daily or several times a week, 12% reported less than once a week, 29% reported a few times a month, and 46% reported that they had rarely observed this behaviour' (Ey & McInnes 2018, p. 95). Most of the educators reported children displaying physical interpersonal harmful sexual behaviours such as touching or mouthing others' genitals and rubbing themselves against a peer (simulating intercourse) and non-physical, interpersonal sexual behaviours such as inviting peers to engage in penetrative sex, to touch their genitals, or to send sexual images of themselves. A minority of educators labelled public sexual expression that is considered socially unacceptable as problematic (Ey & McInnes 2018).

Conclusion

This chapter has demonstrated that children's displays of harmful sexual behaviour are a global phenomenon that is cause for concern. Current research has yielded mixed results about the extent and severity of harmful sexual behaviour, which is likely due to how sexually problematic behaviour is defined and researched as outlined in the introduction. Research concerning harmful sexual behaviour in education settings suggests that children's sexual displays in early childhood are largely age-appropriate sexual expression, but sexual behaviour in primary schools and high school settings appears to be more problematic and even abusive. That this is an issue in need of address is suggested by the fact that children as young as 10 years of age are being criminally charged for sexual crimes and that there are specialised programs to treat children with harmful sexual behaviours. Chapter 4 discusses the impacts of harmful sexual behaviour for the children who display the behaviour as well as for children who are exposed to or are the target of the behaviour.

References

Allen, B 2016, 'Children with sexual behaviour problems: Clinical characteristics and relationship to child maltreatment', *Child Psychiatry & Human Development*, vol. 48, no. 2, pp. 189–199, <https://doi.org/10.1007/s10578-016-0633-8>.

Australian Bureau of Statistics 2017–18, *Recorded crime: Victims, Australia*, Canberra, <www.abs.gov.au/AUSSTATS/abs@.nsf/Lookup/4519.0Main+Features12017-18?OpenDocument>.

Baker, AJL, Gries, L, Schneiderman, M, Parker, R, Archer, M & Friedrich, B 2008, 'Children with problematic sexualised behaviours in the child welfare system', *Child Welfare*, vol. 87, no. 1, pp. 5–27, <http://search.proquest.com/docview/213807752?pq-origsite=gscholar>.

Baker, AJL, Schneiderman, M & Parker, R 2001, 'A survey of problematic sexualized behaviors of children in the New York City child welfare system: Estimates of problem, impact on services, and need for training', *Journal of Child Sexual Abuse*, vol. 10, no. 4, pp. 67–80, <https://doi.org/10.1300/J070v10n04_05>.

Briggs, F 2012, *Child protection: The essential guide for teachers and other professionals whose work involves children*, JoJo Publishing, Docklands, Victoria.

Bromfield, L, Hirte, C, Octoman, O & Katz, I 2017, *Child sexual abuse in Australian institutional contexts 2008–2013: Findings from administrative data*, Sydney, <www.childabuseroyalcommission.gov.au/sites/default/files/file-list/research_report_-_child_sexual_abuse_in_australian_institutional_contexts_2008-13_findings_from_administrative_data_-_causes.pdf>.

Carmody, T 2013, *Taking responsibility: A roadmap for Queensland child protection, report of the Queensland child protection commission of inquiry*, Queensland Government, Brisbane.

Clear, ER, Coker, AL, Cook-Craig, PG, Bush, HM, Garcia, LS, Williams, CM & Fisher, BS 2014, 'Sexual harassment victimization and perpetration among high school students', *Violence Against Women*, vol. 20, no. 10, pp. 1203–1219, <https://doi.org/10.1177/1077801214551287>.

Cox, S, Ey, L, Parkinson, S & Bromfield, L 2018, *Service models for children under 10 with problematic sexual behaviours: An evidence check rapid review brokered by the Sax Institute for the NSW Ministry of Health*, Sydney, <www.health.nsw.gov.au/parvan/sexualassault/Documents/service-models-under10.PDF>.

Davies, SL, Glaser, D & Kossoff, R 2000, 'Children's sexual play and behavior in pre-school settings: Staff's perceptions, reports, and responses', *Child Abuse & Neglect*, vol. 24, no. 10, pp. 1329–1343, <https://doi.org/10.1016/S0145-2134(00)00184-8>.

Debelle, B 2013, *Independent Education Inquiry 2012–2013*, SA Government, Adelaide, <www.saasso.asn.au/wp-content/uploads/2013/11/DebelleInquiry.pdf>.

Department for Education 2018, *Sexual violence and sexual harassment between children in schools and colleges: Advice for governing bodies, proprietors, headteachers, principals, senior leadership teams and designated safeguarding leads*, London, <https://assets.publishing.service.gov.uk/government/uploads/system/uploads/attachment_data/file/719902/Sexual_violence_and_sexual_harassment_between_children_in_schools_and_colleges.pdf>.

El-Murr, A 2017, *Problem sexual behaviours and sexually abusive behaviours in Australian children and young people: A review of available literature*, AIFS, Melbourne, Victoria, <https://aifs.gov.au/cfca/publications/problem-sexual-behaviours-and-sexually-abusive-behaviours-australian-children>.

Ey, L & McInnes, E 2018, 'Educators' observations of children's display of problematic sexual behaviors in educational settings', *Journal of Child Sexual Abuse*, vol. 27, no. 1, pp. 88–105, <https://doi.org/10.1080/10538712.2017.1349855>.

Family and Community Development Committee 2013, *Betrayal of trust: Inquiry into the handling of child abuse by religious and other non-government organisations*, Victoria, <www.parliament.vic.gov.au/file_uploads/Inquiry_into_Handling_of_Abuse_Volume_2_FINAL_web_y78t3Wpb.pdf>.

Forde, L 1999, *Report of the commission of inquiry into child abuse in Queensland institutions*, Queensland Government, Brisbane, <www.qld.gov.au/__data/assets/pdf_file/0023/54509/forde-comminquiry.pdf>.

Friedrich, WN 1997, *Manual for the child sexual behavior inventory*, Psychological Assessment Resources, Odessa, Florida.

Gillander, G 2012, 'Sexual harassment of girls in elementary school: A concealed phenomenon within a heterosexual romantic discourse', *Journal of Interpersonal Violence*, vol. 29, no. 9, pp. 1762–1779, <https://doi.org/10.1177/0886260511430387>.

Gordon, S, Hallahan, K & Henry, D 2002, *Putting the picture together: Inquiry into response by government agencies to complaints of family violence and child abuse in Aboriginal communities*, WA Department of Premier and Cabinet, Perth.

Hart, A, Lane, D & Doherty, G 2017, *Report of the historical institutional abuse inquiry*, United Kingdom, <www.hiainquiry.org/historical-institutional-abuse-inquiry-report-chapters>.

Hill, C & Kearl, H 2011, *Crossing the line: Sexual harassment at school*, Washington, DC, <www.aauw.org/files/2013/02/Crossing-the-Line-Sexual-Harassment-at-School.pdf>.

Johnson, TC 1988, 'Child perpetrators – children who molest other children: Preliminary findings', *Child Abuse & Neglect*, vol. 12, no. 2, pp. 219–229, <https://doi.org/10.1016/0145-2134(88)90030-0>.

Johnson, TC 1989, 'Female child perpetrators: Children who molest other children', *Child Abuse & Neglect*, vol. 13, no. 4, pp. 571–585, <https://doi.org/10.1016/0145-2134(89)90061-6>.

Larsson, I & Svedin, CG 2002, 'Teacher's and parents' reports on 3- to 6-year old children's sexual behaviour – A comparison', *Child Abuse and Neglect*, 26(3), 247–266, <https://doi.org/10.1016/S0145-2134(01)00323-4>.

Layton, R 2003, *Our best investment: A state plan to protect and advance the interests of children*, SA Government, Adelaide, <www.childprotection.sa.gov.au/__data/assets/pdf_file/0003/107274/layton-child-protection-review.pdf>.

Lindblad, F, Gustafsson, PA, Larsson, I & Lundin, B 1995, 'Preschoolers' sexual behaviour at daycare centers: An epidemiological study', *Child Abuse & Neglect*, vol. 10, no. 5, pp. 569–577, <https://doi.org/10.1016/0145-2134(95)00016-2>.

Lussier, P, McCuish, E, Mathesius, J, Corrado, R & Nadeau, D 2017, 'Developmental trajectories of child sexual behaviours on the path of sexual behavioural problems: Evidence from a prospective longitudinal study', *Sexual Abuse*, vol. 30, no. 6, pp. 622–658, <https://doi.org/10.1177/1079063217691963>.

Marina Ajduković, N & Sušac, MR 2013, 'Gender and age differences in prevalence and incidence of child sexual abuse in Croatia', *Croatia Medical Journal*, vol. 53, no. 5, pp. 469–479, <https://doi.org/10.3325/cmj.2013.54.469>.

McDonald, RA, Des Roisers, N, Boniface, G, Owen, S & Buchanan, A 2000, *Restoring dignity: Responding to child abuse in Canadian institutions*, Canada, <http://publications.gc.ca/collections/collection_2008/lcc-cdc/JL2-7-2000-2E.pdf>.

McKibbin, G 2017, 'Preventing harmful sexual behaviour and child sexual exploitation for children & young people living in residential care: A scoping review in the Australian context', *Children and Youth Services Review*, vol. 82, pp. 373–382, <https://doi.org/10.1016/j.childyouth.2017.10.008>.

Mesman, GR, Harper, SL, Edge, NA, Brandt, TW & Pemberton, JL 2019, 'Problematic sexual behaviour in children', *Journal of Pediatric Health Care*, vol. 33, no. 3, pp. 323–331.

Moore, T, McArthur, M, Death, J, Tilbury, C & Rochea, S 2017, 'Young people's views on safety and preventing abuse and harm in residential care: "It's got to be better than home"', *Children and Youth Services Review*, vol. 81, pp. 212–219, <https://doi.org/10.1016/j.childyouth.2017.08.010>.

Mullighan, E 2008, *Children in state care commission of inquiry: Allegations of sexual abuse and death from criminal conduct*, SA Government, Adelaide, <www.childprotection.sa.gov.au/__data/assets/pdf_file/0011/107201/children-in-state-care-commission-of-inquiry-introducation.pdf>.

Murphy, FD, Buckley, H & Joyce, L 2005, *The ferns report, presented by the ferns inquiry to the minister for health and children*, Dublin, <www.bishop-accountability.org/ferns/>.

Murphy, Y, Mangan, I & O'Niell, H 2009, R*eport by commission of investigation into Catholic archdiocese of Dublin*, Dublin, <www.justice.ie/en/JELR/Cloyne_Rpt.pdf/Files/Cloyne_Rpt.pdf>.

Murphy, Y, Mangan, I & O'Niell, H 2010, *Report by commission of investigation into Catholic diocese of Cloyne*, Dublin, <www.justice.ie/en/JELR/Pages/Cloyne-Rpt>.

National Center for Juvenile Justice 2012, *National report series: Juvenile arrests 2012*, United States, <www.ojjdp.gov/pubs/248513.pdf>.

National Society for the Prevention of Cruelty to Children 2018, *"Is this sexual abuse?" NSPCC helplines report: Peer sexual abuse*, London, <https://learning.nspcc.org.uk/research-resources/2018/is-this-sexual-abuse/>.

New South Wales Legislative Council 2017, *Child protection*. General purpose standing committee No. 2, NSW Parliament, Sydney, <www.parliament.nsw.gov.au/lcdocs/inquiries/2396/Final%20report%20-%20Child%20protection.pdf>.

Norman, RE, Byambaa, M, De, R, Butchart, A, Scott, J & Vos, T 2012, 'The long-term health consequences of child physical abuse, emotional abuse, and neglect: A systematic review and meta-analysis', *PLoS Med*, vol. 9, no. 11, p. e1001349, <https://doi.org/10.1371/journal.pmed.1001349>.

NSPCC 2018, *Is this sexual abuse? NSPCC helplines report: Peer sexual abuse*, London, <https://learning.nspcc.org.uk/media/1032/nspcc-helplines-report-peer-sexual-abuse.pdf>.

NSPCC 2019, *Harmful sexual behaviour framework: An evidence-informed operational framework for children and young people displaying harmful sexual behaviour*, London, <www.icmec.org/wp-content/uploads/2019/04/harmful-sexual-behaviour-framework.pdf>.

Nyland, M 2016, *The life they deserve: Child protection systems royal commission report*, Government of South Australia, Adelaide, <https://agdsa.govcms.gov.au/sites/default/files/complete_report_child_protection_systems_royal_commission_report.pdf?acsf_files_redirect>.

O'Brien, W 2010, *Australia's response to sexualised or sexually abuse behaviours in children and young people*, Canberra, <http://dro.deakin.edu.au/eserv/DU:30065114/obrien-australias-2010.pdf>.

O'Halloran, P 2011, *Final report: Select committee on child protection*, Parliament of Tasmania, Select Committee on Child Protection, Hobart, <www.parliament.tas.gov.au/ctee/House/childprotection.htm>.

Parliament UK 2016, *Sexual harassment and sexual violence in schools*, London, <https://publications.parliament.uk/pa/cm201617/cmselect/cmwomeq/91/9105.htm#_idTextAnchor011>.

Royal Commission into Institutional Responses to Child Sexual Abuse 2016, *Institutional responses to child sexual abuse in out-of-home care: Consultation paper*, Sydney, <www.childabuseroyalcommission.gov.au/consultation-papers>.

Royal Commission into Institutional Responses to Child Sexual Abuse 2017a, *Final report: Preface and executive summary*, ACT, <www.childabuseroyalcommission.gov.au/sites/default/files/final_report_-_preface_and_executive_summary.pdf>.

Royal Commission into Institutional Responses to Child Sexual Abuse 2017b, *Final report: Volume 10, children with harmful sexual behaviours*, <www.childabuseroyalcommission.gov.au/sites/default/files/final_report_-_volume_10_children_with_harmful_sexual_behaviours.pdf>.

36 Children's harmful sexual behaviour

Royal Commission into Institutional Responses to Child Sexual Abuse 2017c, *Final report: Volume 12, Contemporary out-of-home care*, ACT, <www.childabuseroyal commission.gov.au/sites/default/files/final_report_-_volume_12_contemporary_ out-of-home_care.pdf>.

Royal Commission into Institutional Responses to Child Sexual Abuse 2017d, *Final report: Volume 13, Schools*, ACT, <www.childabuseroyalcommission. gov.au/particular-institutions>.

Royal Commission into Institutional Responses to Child Sexual Abuse 2017e, *Final report: Volume 14, Sport, recreation, arts, culture, community and hobby groups*, ACT, <www.childabuseroyalcommission.gov.au/sites/default/files/final_report_-_ volume_14_sport_recreation_arts_culture_community_and_hobby_groups.pdf>.

Royal Commission into Institutional Responses to Child Sexual Abuse 2017f, *Final report: Volume 16, Religious institutions, book 1*, ACT, <www.childabuse royalcommission.gov.au/sites/default/files/final_report_-_volume_16_religious_ institutions_book_1.pdf>.

Royal Commission into Institutional Responses to Child Sexual Abuse 2017g, *Final report: Volume 15, Contemporary detention environments*, ACT, <www.child abuseroyalcommission.gov.au/sites/default/files/final_report_-_volume_15_ contemporary_detention_environments.pdf>.

Royal Commission into Institutional Responses to Child Sexual Abuse 2017h, *Identifying and disclosing child sexual abuse*, Sydney, <www.childabuse royalcommission.gov.au/research>.

Ryan, S 2009, *Commission to inquire into child abuse*, Dublin, <www.childabuse commission.ie/rpt/pdfs/>.

Senate Community Affairs Reference Committee 2001, *Lost innocence: Righting the record: Report on child migration*, Canberra, <www.aph.gov.au/Parliamentary_ Business/Committees/Senate/Community_Affairs/completed_inquiries/1999-02/ child_migrat/report/index.htm>.

Senate Community Affairs Reference Committee 2004, *Forgotten Australians: Report on Australians who experienced institutional or out-of-home care as children*, Canberra, <www.aph.gov.au/Parliamentary_Business/Committees/Senate/ Community_Affairs/Completed_inquiries/2004-07/inst_care/report/index>.

Shaw, JA, Lewis, JE, Loeb, A, Rosado, J & Rodriguez, RA 2000, 'Child on child sexual abuse: Psychological perspectives', *Child Abuse & Neglect*, vol. 24, no. 12, pp. 1591–1600, <https://doi.org/10.1016/S0145-2134(00)00212-X>.

Shlonsky, A, Albers, B, Tolliday, D, Wilson, S, Norvell, J & Kissinger, L 2017, *Rapid evidence assessment: Current best evidence in the therapeutic treatment of children with problem or harmful sexual behaviours, and children who have sexually offended*, Sydney, <www.childabuseroyalcommission.gov.au/policy- and-research/our-research/publishedresearch/therapeutic-treatment-of-children- with-problem-or>.

Sickmund, M & Puzzanchera, C 2014, *Juvenile offenders and victims: 2014 national report*, Pittsburg, <www.ojjdp.gov/ojstatbb/nr2014/downloads/NR2014.pdf>.

Silovsky, J & Niec, L 2002, 'Characteristics of young children with sexual behaviour problems: A pilot study', *Child Maltreatment*, vol. 7, no. 3, pp. 187–197, <https://doi.org/10.1177/1077559502007003002>.

Silovsky, J, Niec, L, Bard, D & Hecht, DB 2007, 'Treatment for preschool children with interpersonal sexual behaviour problems: A pilot study', *Journal of Clinical Child & Adolescent Psychology*, vol. 36, no. 3, pp. 378–391, <https://doi.org/10.1080/15374410701444330>.

Turner, HA, Finkelhor, D, Hamby, SL, Shattuck, A & Ormrod, RK 2011, 'Specifying type and location of peer victimization in a national sample of children and youth', *Journal of Youth and Adolescence*, vol. 40, no. 8, pp. 1052–1067.

Victoria Parliament Family & Community Development Committee 2013, *Betrayal of trust: Inquiry into the handling of child abuse by religious and other nongovernment organisations*, Victoria Parliament, Melbourne.

Wild, R & Anderson, P 2007, *Ampe akelyernemane meke mekarle: 'little children are sacred': Report of the Northern Territory board of inquiry into the protection of Aboriginal children from sexual abuse*, Northern Territory Government, Darwin, <www.inquirysaac.nt.gov.au/pdf/bipacsa_final_report.pdf>.

4 Aftermath and impacts of harmful sexual behaviour

Introduction

The psychological, social, and economic costs of child sexual assault and harmful sexual behaviour are high. The global economic impacts and costs resulting from physical, psychological, and sexual violence against children are estimated at $7 trillion (Pereznieto, Montes, Langston, & Routier 2014). In Australia, the potential flow-on costs from children's harmful sexual behaviour are significant. Australia spends at least $28.6 billion per year, excluding capital expenditure, supporting people with mental illness (Medibank Private Limited and Nous Group 2013); approximately $775 million on sexual assault (Smith, Jorna, Sweeney, & Fuller 2014); and $5.2 billion on family support services, protective intervention services, and out-of-home care services (Australian Government Productivity Commission 2018). Alongside the broader social and economic impacts, children's harmful sexual behaviours are concerning for several reasons. Firstly, research has identified a wide range of adverse effects on psychological health, such as internalising and externalising disorders (Maker, Kemmelmeier, & Peterson 2001; Sperry & Gilbert 2005), impacts on physical health, neurobiological development, interpersonal relationships, connection to culture and sexual identity, adverse developmental trajectories, and harmful behavioural or conduct problems later in life (O'Brien 2010; Shlonsky et al. 2017). This chapter explores the impacts on children who have experienced unwanted sexual encounters and the impacts on children who have exhibited harmful sexual behaviour.

Impacts of harmful sexual behaviour for children who have experienced unwanted sexual encounters

'An unwanted sexual act by another child has the same psychological impact on the victim as if the abuse were by an adult' (O'Brien 2010,

Impacts of harmful sexual behaviour 39

p. 23). Additionally, the trauma impact and behavioural outcomes for children who have been sexually abused by another child were not significantly different from those who had been abused by an adult (Shaw, Lewis, Loeb, Rosado, & Rodriguez 2000). Therefore, the literature presented discusses the impact of child sexual abuse. Although not all harmful sexual behaviour directed at other children is considered sexually abusive (O'Brien 2008, 2010; Royal Commission into Institutional Responses to Child Sexual Abuse 2017b), there is no predictability for how unwanted sexual encounters will affect children.

There are multiple factors which can influence the ways that children are affected by sexual abuse. The severity or type of impact children who have been sexually abused experience depends on the type, duration, and frequency of the abuse; the child's relationship to the perpetrator; the child's characteristics (i.e. age, gender, disability); the child's previous experiences (i.e. prior maltreatment and experiences with disclosure of abuse); and children's resilience or support networks (Royal Commission into Institutional Responses to Child Sexual Abuse 2017a; The Australian Child & Adolescent Trauma Loss and Grief Network no date). Children who have been sexually abused or been a victim of unwanted sexual contact can suffer across many areas of their lives, and the impacts can be lifelong. The Adverse Childhood Experiences study, performed by Felitti et al. (1998), collected health data from more than 17,000 adults in the United States and then surveyed them on their childhood experiences of psychological, physical, or sexual abuse; violence against their mother; living with substance abusers; or family members who were mentally ill, suicidal, or ever imprisoned. The study identified that those who had experienced more than four of these events were much more likely to experience alcoholism, smoking, drug abuse, depression, suicidality, poor self-rated health, high numbers of sexual intercourse partners, sexually transmitted disease, limited physical inactivity, and severe obesity. These in turn resulted in increased rates of heart disease, cancer, chronic lung disease, skeletal fractures, and liver disease.

The Royal Commission into Institutional Responses to Child Sexual Abuse (2017a) heard from 6,412 survivors of child sexual abuse in institutions (Table 4.1). The majority (94.9%) reported that they developed mental health issues and more than half of the survivors suffered relationship problems (67.6%) and education and/or economic issues (55.7%). Almost a quarter of the victims developed harmful sexual behaviour (24.2%).

Trauma

It is widely recognised that child sexual abuse is associated with the development of trauma symptoms (Cashmore & Shackel 2013; Cook et al.

40 Impacts of harmful sexual behaviour

Table 4.1 Impacts of child sexual abuse on survivors, information from private sessions, May 2013–May 2017 (Royal Commission into Institutional Responses to Child Sexual Abuse 2017a, p. 75)

Impact	Number affected (6,412 survivors)	Proportion %
Mental health issues	6,088	94.9
Relationship issues	4,332	67.6
Education and/or economic issues	3,569	55.7
Sexual behaviour issues	1,554	24.2
Involvement in crime	1,456	22.7
Physical health issues	461	7.2
Direct consequences (pregnancy, transmitted infection, injury)	440	6.9
Other	32	0.5

Note: Percentages are provided as a proportion of those survivors who provided information in private sessions about the impacts of child sexual abuse.

2005; Gaskill & Perry 2012; O'Brien 2010; Royal Commission into Institutional Responses to Child Sexual Abuse 2017a; The Australian Child & Adolescent Trauma, Loss and Grief Network no date). According to Cook et al., 'Children exposed to complex trauma often experience lifelong problems that place them at risk for additional trauma exposure and cumulative impairment (eg. psychiatric and addictive disorders; chronic medical illness; legal, vocational, and family problems)' (2005, p. 390). Traumatising experiences can cause lasting changes in the endocrine, autonomic, and central nervous systems (Royal Commission into Institutional Responses to Child Sexual Abuse 2017a). Gaskill and Perry (2012) explain that child sexual abuse and trauma impact the development of the brain; the lower-brain regions (brainstem and diencephalon) and the higher-brain regions (limbic and cortex) are shaped by nature (genetics) and nurture (environmental influences). During the development process, children's brains gather information through their senses, process and integrate the information, store the information, and act on it from both their internal (blood, glucose, CO_2 levels, and arterial pressure) and external environment (auditory, visual, tactile, olfactory, gustatory, vestibular, and proprioceptive). Neural pathways are continually developing in response to the child's internal and environmental stimuli and the more frequent the experiences, the stronger these neural pathways become. The brain development of children living with trauma adapts in response to living with constant threat. This means that children often do not have conscious control over their actions or emotions and these responses become automatic (Gaskill & Perry 2012).

Mental health

Much of the scholarly literature identifies that children who have been sexually abused are at risk of developing mental illness, including depression, anxiety, post-traumatic stress disorder (PTSD), eating disorders, drug or alcohol abuse, personality disorders, dissociative disorder, and psychotic disorders, such as schizophrenia and delusional disorder (Cashmore & Shackel 2013; Fergusson, McLeod, & Horwood 2013; Royal Commission into Institutional Responses to Child Sexual Abuse 2017a). Penetrative child sexual abuse presents a greater risk factor for developing psychotic disorders (Cashmore & Shackel 2013). The most concerning of the forms of mental illness related to child sexual abuse are suicide ideation, suicide attempts, and actual suicides (Cashmore & Shackel 2013; Fergusson et al. 2013; Royal Commission into Institutional Responses to Child Sexual Abuse 2017a). Emotional and behavioural issues related to child sexual abuse include low self-esteem and self-worth, negative attributions, shame, humiliation, guilt, self-blame, a sense of powerlessness and helplessness, grief, sleeping difficulties, nightmares, conduct disorder, harmful sexual behaviour, and aggressive behaviours (Briggs 2012; Cashmore & Shackel 2013; Royal Commission into Institutional Responses to Child Sexual Abuse 2017a).

Interpersonal relationships

As identified by the Australian Childhood Foundation (2006), traumatised children have difficulty developing trusting relationships. This lack of trust can extend into their adult lives and affect their future relationships. The Royal Commission into Institutional Responses to Child Sexual Abuse (2017a) and Fisher, Goldsmith, Hurcombe, and Soares (2017) found that many survivors of childhood sexual abuse had difficulties developing and maintaining intimate relationships, had poor relationship stability, and suffered sexual problems or dysfunction (Cashmore & Shackel 2013; Fisher et al. 2017). Others reported risky sexual behaviours, such as engaging in unprotected sex, having multiple partners, engaging in sex work, and engaging in sexual activity from an early age (Cashmore & Shackel 2013; Fergusson et al. 2013; Royal Commission into Institutional Responses to Child Sexual Abuse 2017a). Child sexual abuse has also been associated with victims experiencing interpersonal violence (Fisher et al. 2017; Royal Commission into Institutional Responses to Child Sexual Abuse 2017a) and revictimisation (Maker et al. 2001).

The emotional problems arising from child sexual abuse and the difficulty in developing trusting relationships affect attachment. Traumatised children often have poor internal working models and poor attachments

(Australian Childhood Foundation 2006). Research demonstrates that only 16.59% of 247 Irish adult survivors of institutional abuse were able to form secure adult attachments (Fitzpatrick et al. 2010). This then makes it more difficult for individuals who have grown up with trauma to develop secure attachments with their own children. Child sexual abuse victims have been found to have less satisfying relationships, are less likely to marry, more likely to divorce (Royal Commission into Institutional Responses to Child Sexual Abuse 2017a), and are at a greater risk of isolation and loneliness (Cashmore & Shackel 2013; Royal Commission into Institutional Responses to Child Sexual Abuse 2017a).

Sexual identity

Research has identified that some children who have been sexually abused develop uncertainty about their sexual identity. This was more prevalent in boys (Cashmore & Shackel 2013; Fisher et al. 2017; Royal Commission into Institutional Responses to Child Sexual Abuse 2017a). The sexual 'abuse caused them confusion about whether they were gay, lesbian, heterosexual, or bisexual' (Royal Commission into Institutional Responses to Child Sexual Abuse 2017a, p. 123). Some boys who reported impacts on their sexual identity felt confused if their body responded physically to the abuse, such as if they obtained an erection or ejaculated during the abuse (Royal Commission into Institutional Responses to Child Sexual Abuse 2017a).

Physical health

As outlined earlier, trauma in early childhood impacts the developing architecture of the brain. Traumatised children often have overdeveloped regions in the brain involved in anxiety and fear responses and underdeveloped regions impacting their ability to self-regulate behaviour, emotions, and thoughts (Royal Commission into Institutional Responses to Child Sexual Abuse 2017a). General physical health is poorer for child sexual abuse victims (Fergusson et al. 2013) which has been correlated with a complex matrix of inter-relationships among other impacts. For example, they may experience increased risk of developing mental illness or drug and alcohol addictions, and engaging in risky behaviour can increase risks of cancer, sexually transmitted infections, and heart disease (Cashmore & Shackel 2013); Felitti et al. 1998).

Physical injury resulting from violent or physical sexual abuse can include bruising and anal or vaginal tears (Briggs 2012; Fisher et al. 2017; Royal Commission into Institutional Responses to Child Sexual Abuse 2017a).

Impacts of harmful sexual behaviour 43

Long-term physical impacts can include chronic illness (Cashmore & Shackel 2013; Fisher et al. 2017); bowel, bladder, and genital dysfunction; and inability to have children as a result of acute physical injuries to the genital area and other organs (Royal Commission into Institutional Responses to Child Sexual Abuse 2017a). Other diseases correlated with child sexual abuse include lung problems, heart disease, liver disease, digestive system problems, musculoskeletal problems, obesity/high body mass index (BMI), diabetes, arthritis, immune system problems, non-epileptic seizures, and cancer (Fisher et al. 2017).

Children who have been sexually abused are at risk of contracting sexually transmitted infections, or having unplanned pregnancies, miscarriages, and abortions (Cashmore & Shackel 2013; Royal Commission into Institutional Responses to Child Sexual Abuse 2017a). Some of the infections children are at risk of contracting include chlamydia, herpes, gonorrhoea, syphilis, genital warts, hepatitis C, and HIV (Briggs 2012; Royal Commission into Institutional Responses to Child Sexual Abuse 2017a). Some of these diseases can have devastating and lifelong effects. For example:

> BXA, giving evidence in the 'Sporting Clubs and Institutions' case study, told us how she was raped by her soccer coach when she was aged eight. She was diagnosed as HIV positive shortly before her 15th birthday, and believes she contracted it from the perpetrator. BXA told us about the ongoing effects of the HIV:
>
>> The sexual abuse that I experienced has had a massive, irreversible impact on my life. I live with a constant reminder of the abuse every single day of my life because of the HIV. Sometimes I want to forget that I have HIV and I have gone through times where I have not taken my medication, which I now know would be a really easy way to kill myself.... You can get really sick from the HIV medication itself, although I am more used to it now. I can still get a bad reaction whenever they change the dose or the type of medication. My liver has been affected and I have had really bad itchy eyes like with conjunctivitis. I have also had to have brain tests because the chemicals affect your brain.
>> (Royal Commission into Institutional Responses to Child Sexual Abuse 2017a, p. 118)

Education, employment, and economic security

Research has identified that children who have been sexually abused have lower levels of educational engagement and attainment (Briggs 2012;

Fisher et al. 2017; O'Brien 2010; Royal Commission into Institutional Responses to Child Sexual Abuse 2017a). The emotional and psychological impacts on children who have been sexually abused affect children's ability to concentrate, self-regulate, and engage in schooling activities (Briggs 2012; Fisher et al. 2017; Royal Commission into Institutional Responses to Child Sexual Abuse 2017a). Deterioration in school performance often begins immediately after the abuse occurs (Royal Commission into Institutional Responses to Child Sexual Abuse 2017a). Children may begin to avoid school, particularly if the abuse occurred there (Briggs 2012). Some adult survivors who reported being sexually abused by an adult or a child at school reported school avoidance and feelings of fear, anxiety, anger, and distrust whilst at school. Survivors of child sexual abuse reported low levels of school engagement as a result of truancy, health problems, exclusions, or suspension caused by behavioural problems, and dropping out (Fisher et al. 2017; Royal Commission into Institutional Responses to Child Sexual Abuse 2017a). These disruptions caused significant gaps in knowledge and further affected their ability to attend higher education and seek employment (Fergusson et al. 2013; Fisher et al. 2017; Royal Commission into Institutional Responses to Child Sexual Abuse 2017a). A small number of survivors discussed focusing on their education as a means to try to ignore or forget the abuse and increase their job opportunities (Fisher et al. 2017; Royal Commission into Institutional Responses to Child Sexual Abuse 2017a).

Child sexual abuse has been 'associated with increased unemployment and time out of the labour market; increased receipt of welfare benefits; income and financial instability; and reduced incomes' (Fisher et al. 2017, p. 98). Some of the factors correlated with the impacts on employment opportunities include mental illness, drug or alcohol abuse, low self-esteem, trust issues, physical illness, stress-related outbursts, and low educational attainment (Fisher et al. 2017; Royal Commission into Institutional Responses to Child Sexual Abuse 2017a). Homelessness was a common theme for child sexual abuse victims, with several discussing times in their life where they lived on the street (Fisher et al. 2017; Royal Commission into Institutional Responses to Child Sexual Abuse 2017a).

It is important to note that although there is a broad body of research that explores the impact of child sexual abuse that has identified various significant detrimental outcomes, not all children will be impacted in these ways (Royal Commission into Institutional Responses to Child Sexual Abuse 2017a). Children who have developed resilience and who have a strong and supportive network have a greater opportunity to live a healthy life (Evertsz & Miller 2012; Royal Commission into Institutional Responses to Child Sexual Abuse 2017a).

Impacts of harmful sexual behaviour for children who display the behaviour

As discussed in more detail in the next chapter, there is no single factor that causes children to develop harmful sexual behaviour (Chaffin et al. 2008; Evertsz & Miller 2012; Royal Commission into Institutional Responses to Child Sexual Abuse 2017b; Staiger 2005). The risk factors for developing problem sexual behaviours include being sexually, physically, or emotionally abused; being neglected; living with domestic violence, substance abuse, or mental illness; chronic trauma; psychological disorders, such as attention-deficit/hyperactivity disorder (ADHD); behavioural and social disorders; and intellectual disability (Chaffin et al. 2008; Evertsz & Miller 2012; Royal Commission into Institutional Responses to Child Sexual Abuse 2017b; Silovsky & Niec 2002; Staiger 2005). As such, these children are at risk of experiencing the same impacts as outlined in the previous section, as most have been traumatised.

Research has demonstrated that children who display harmful sexual behaviour have higher levels of depression and anxiety; disruptive behaviour problems; behavioural disorders; developmental delay; and learning disorders (Chaffin et al. 2008; Evertsz & Miller 2012; Staiger 2005). There are wide-ranging implications for the child's social, emotional, and behavioural development, as well as for their long-term adjustment (Silovsky & Niec 2002). Staiger (2005) states that children who engage in harmful sexual behaviour lacked understanding and had difficulty in developing and maintaining peer relationships. She reported that children with harmful sexual behaviour had limited understanding of personal boundaries and were vulnerable to peer isolation. Conversely, children's indiscriminate friendliness and inability to understand boundaries may place them at increased risk of being victimised (Silovsky & Niec 2002). Shlonsky et al. (2017) note that children who display sexual behaviour are at an increased risk of being sexually exploited.

When children display harmful sexual behaviour it can been seen as 'shocking' and 'socially unacceptable' because children are seen as innocent (Staiger 2005). Children are at risk of being stigmatised and socially rejected by their peers, teachers, parents in the school, and the broader community. The lack of understanding about harmful sexual behaviour may lead to adults labelling children who have harmful sexual behaviour as perpetrators, reinforcing the stigma. Children who are seen as 'bad', 'unacceptable', or a 'social burden' are at risk of poor identity formation which could potentially result in children adopting the behaviours that befit the label (Berk 2013). It is important to only label the behaviour and not the child.

46 *Impacts of harmful sexual behaviour*

As discussed further in Chapter 6, from a legal perspective, children can be criminally convicted in Australia for sexual assault and related offences as young as 10 years of age (Royal Commission into Institutional Responses to Child Sexual Abuse 2017b). Despite considerable concern about children's harmful sexual behaviour progressing to adult sexual offending, 'the available evidence suggests that children with harmful sexual behaviour are at very low risk to commit future sex offences, especially if provided with appropriate treatment' (Chaffin et al. 2008, p. 2).

Conclusion

The social, economic, and health costs of harmful sexual behaviour are significant. The potential impacts for children who have experienced unwanted sexual encounters are as damaging to the child as when the abuse was perpetrated by an adult. These impacts can have lifelong effects on the children's psychological, emotional, and physical health, as well as their social and economic stability. Children who display harmful sexual behaviour are vulnerable to these, and to other impacts associated with the stigma attached to these behaviours. It is important that educators recognise the impacts for all children involved and respond to the behaviour rather than labelling the child.

References

The Australian Child & Adolescent Trauma, LGN no date, *The impact of abuse and neglect on children*, <www.google.com.au/url?sa=t&rct=j&q=&esrc=s&source=web&cd=3&ved=0ahUKEwjcnNHe7MLPAhVCp5QKHXWTBkgQFgg2MAI&url=http%3A%2F%2Fearlytraumagrief.anu.edu.au%2Ffiles%2FThe%2520impact%2520of%2520abuse%2520and%2520neglect%2520on%2520children_2.pdf&usg=AFQjCNHHgS6mgaZSXE123mBksYfbIuvOrQ>.

Australian Childhood Foundation 2006, *Responding to children who have experienced abuse related trauma: Ideas for school-based treatment*, Richmond, Victoria, <https://professionals.childhood.org.au/app/uploads/2018/08/SMART-Discussion-Paper-1-1.pdf>.

Australian Government Productivity Commission 2018, *Report on government services: Child protection services*, Melbourne, Victoria, <www.pc.gov.au/research/ongoing/report-on-government>.

Berk, L 2013, *Child development*, 9th edn, Pearson, Boston.

Briggs, F 2012, *Child protection: The essential guide for teachers and other professionals whose work involves children*, Jo-Jo Publishing, Docklands, Victoria.

Cashmore, J & Shackel, R 2013, *The long-term effects of child sexual abuse*, The Australian Institute of Family Studies, Melbourne, <https://aifs.gov.au/cfca/sites/default/files/cfca/pubs/papers/a143161/cfca11.pdf>.

Chaffin, M, Berliner, L, Block, R, Johnson, TC, Friedrich, WN, Louis, DG, Lyon, TD, Page, IJ, Prescott, DS & Silovsky, JF 2008, 'Report of the ATSA task force on children with sexual behaviour problems', *Child Maltreatment*, vol. 13, no. 2, pp. 199–218.

Cook, A, Spinazzola, J, Ford, J, Lanktree, C, Blaustein, M, Cloitre, M, DeRosa, R, Hubbard, R, Kagan, R, Liautaud, J, Mallah, K, Olafson, E & van der Kolk, B 2005, 'Complex trauma in children and adolescents', *Psychiatric Annals*, vol. 35, no. 5, pp. 390–398.

Evertsz, J & Miller, R 2012, *Children with problem sexual behaviours and their families: Best interests case practice model: Specialist practice resource*, Victorian Government Department of Human Services, Melbourne, <www.cpmanual.vic.gov.au/sites/default/files/Children%20problem%20sexual%20behaviours%20specialist%20practice%20resource%202012%203013%20.pdf>.

Felitti, VJ, Anda, RF, Nordenberg, D, Williamson, D, Spitz, AM, Edwards, V & Marks, JS 1998, 'Relationship of childhood abuse and household dysfunction to many of the leading causes of death in adults', *American Journal of Preventive Medicine*, vol. 14, no. 4, pp. 245–258, <https://doi.org/10.1016/S0749-3797(98)00017-8>.

Fergusson, D, McLeod, G & Horwood, L 2013, 'Childhood sexual abuse and adult developmental outcomes: Findings from a 30-year longitudinal study in New Zealand', *Child Abuse & Neglect*, vol. 37, no. 9, pp. 664–674.

Fisher, C, Goldsmith, A, Hurcombe, R & Soares, C 2017, *The impacts of child sexual abuse: A rapid evidence assessment*, United Kingdom, <www.iicsa.org.uk/key-documents/1534/view/iicsa-impacts-child-sexual-abuse-rapid-evidence-assessment-full-report-english.pdf>.

Fitzpatrick, M, Carr, A, Dooley, B, Flanagan-Howard, R, Flanagan, E, Tierney, K, White, M, Daly, M, Shevlin, M & Egan, J 2010, 'Profiles of adult survivors of severe sexual, physical and emotional institutional abuse in Ireland', *Child Abuse Review*, vol. 19, no. 6, pp. 387–404.

Gaskill, RL & Perry, BD 2012, 'Child sexual abuse, traumatic experiences and their effect on the developing brain', in P Goodyear-Brown (ed), *Handbook of child sexual abuse: Identification, assessment and treatment*, Wiley, New York, pp. 29–49.

Maker, AH, Kemmelmeier, M & Peterson, C 2001, 'Child sexual abuse, peer sexual abuse, and sexual assault in adulthood: A multi-risk model of revictimization', *Journal of Traumatic Stress*, vol. 14, no. 2, pp. 351–368.

Medibank Private Limited and Nous Group 2013, *The case for mental health reform in Australia: A review of expenditure and system design*, Lane Cove, NSW, <www.medibank.com.au/Client/Documents/Pdfs/The_Case_for_Mental_Health_Reform_in_Australia.pdf>.

O'Brien, W 2008, *Problem sexual behaviour in children: A review of the literature*, Australian Crime Commission, Canberra, ACT.

48 Impacts of harmful sexual behaviour

O'Brien, W 2010, *Australia's response to sexualised or sexually abuse behaviours in children and young people*, Australian Crime Commission, Canberra, ACT <http://dro.deakin.edu.au/eserv/DU:30065114/obrien-australias-2010.pdf>.

Pereznieto, P, Montes, A, Langston, L & Routier, S 2014, *The costs and economic impact of violence against children*, London <www.odi.org/sites/odi.org.uk/files/odi-assets/publications-opinion-files/9177.pdf>.

Royal Commission into Institutional Responses to Child Sexual Abuse 2017a, *Final report: Volume 10, children with harmful sexual behaviours*, Sydney, <www.childabuseroyalcommission.gov.au/sites/default/files/final_report_-_volume_10_children_with_harmful_sexual_behaviours.pdf>.

Royal Commission into Institutional Responses to Child Sexual Abuse 2017b, *Final report: Impacts*, The Commission, Sydney, <www.childabuseroyal commission.gov.au/sites/default/files/final_report_-_volume_3_impacts.pdf>.

Shaw, JA, Lewis, JE, Loeb, A, Rosado, J & Rodriguez, RA 2000, 'Child on child sexual abuse: Psychological perspectives', *Child Abuse & Neglect*, vol. 24, no. 12, pp. 1591–1600.

Shlonsky, A, Albers, B, Tolliday, D, Wilson, S, Norvell, J & Kissinger, L 2017, *Rapid evidence assessment: Current best evidence in the therapeutic treatment of children with problem or harmful sexual behaviours, and children who have sexually offended*, Royal Commission into Institutional Responses to Child Sexual Abuse, Sydney, <www.childabuseroyalcommission.gov.au/policy-and-research/our-research/publishedresearch/therapeutic-treatment-of-children-with-problem-or>.

Silovsky, J & Niec, L 2002, 'Characteristics of young children with sexual behaviour problems: A pilot study', *Child Maltreatment*, vol. 7, no. 3, pp. 187–197.

Smith, R, Jorna, P, Sweeney, J & Fuller, G 2014, *Counting the costs of crime in Australia: A 2011 estimate*, Research and public policy series, no. 129, Canberra, <https://aic.gov.au/publications/rpp/rpp129>.

Sperry, DM & Gilbert, BO 2005, 'Child peer sexual abuse: Preliminary data on outcomes and disclosure experiences,' *Child Abuse and Neglect*, vol. 29 no. 8, pp. 889–904, doi:10.1016/j.chiabu.2004.12.011.

Staiger, P 2005, *Children who engage in problem sexual behaviours: Context, characteristics and treatment: A review of the literature*, Australian Childhood Foundation and Deakin University, Melbourne.

5 Influences on harmful sexual behaviour
Child characteristics, familial and social context

Introduction

There is no single explanation for what may cause the development of harmful sexual behaviour; however, there are characteristics and circumstances which heighten children's vulnerabilities. This chapter reviews scholarly literature around children's individual characteristics that make them vulnerable to sexual exploitation, which is a recognised factor in the development of harmful sexual behaviour, as well as their difficulties understanding appropriate sexual expression. It also examines aspects of children's environments that have been evidenced as increasing children's vulnerability to developing harmful sexual behaviours. The chapter aims to provide insight into influencing factors for educators and other professionals whose work involves supporting children's wellbeing.

The factors that affect young children's sexual behaviours are the subject of ongoing research, principally drawn from studies involving children who have been identified as engaging in these behaviours. Factors that have been identified that may contribute to children learning or acting out harmful sexual behaviours include a history of child maltreatment, trauma or disadvantage, exposure to domestic violence, exposure to sexually explicit material or pornography, mental health issues, experiences of living in out-of-home care, and family dysfunction or disruptions. There are strong and persistent links between sexual abuse and children displaying sexually harmful behaviours (Briggs 2012; Shlonsky et al. 2017).

The hidden nature of child exploitation and other forms of child maltreatment presents a challenge to the search for antecedent factors when a child is identified as displaying harmful sexual behaviours. One consequence is that research into pre-pubescent children's harmful sexual behaviours is unable to conclusively discriminate between those children who have a history of abuse and those who do not (Johnson 1988, 1989; Shaw, Lewis, Loeb, Rosado, & Rodriguez 2000; Silovsky & Niec 2002; Sperry & Gilbert 2005). Other research has sampled children with harmful sexual behaviours who have been taken into the child protection system because of a history of some kind of abuse or neglect (Baker et al. 2008). Numerous studies have confirmed the prevalence of sexual abuse as a risk factor for harmful sexual behaviours but have also found no known history of sexual abuse in a proportion of children exhibiting harmful sexual behaviours (Bonner, Walker, & Berliner 1999; Friedrich 1993; Friedrich, Baker et al. 2005; Friedrich et al. 2001; Friedrich, Gully, & Trane 2005).

Smith, Lindsey, Bohora, and Silovsky (2019) contend that there are multiple pathways into the development of harmful sexual behaviours. In their study of intrusive sexual behaviours (ISB) as a subset of harmful sexual behaviours involving children touching others' private parts or attempting penetrative acts, Smith et al. (2019) cite research by Friedrich, Davies, Feher, and Wright (2003) which proposed that ISB by children aged 2 to 12 could be linked to four types of experiences. These were (a) exposure to sexual behaviour and sexually explicit content, (b) exposure to coercive or violent behaviour, (c) family adversity, and (d) child vulnerabilities relating to expressive and behavioural difficulties, including symptoms of posttraumatic stress disorder (PTSD). The divide between these categories derives from research analysis rather than discrete boundaries or single experiences.

Children who engage in harmful sexual behaviours have often experienced multiple or cumulative types of harm to their development as a result of various forms of child maltreatment (Chaffin 2008; Tarren-Sweeney 2008) and exposure to parental violence (Kambouropoulos 2005; Merrick, Litrownick, Everson, & Cox 2008; Silovsky & Niec 2002) over time.

Streeck-Fischer and van der Kolk (2000) identify that cumulative exposures to traumatic experiences impede children's neuro-typical development and can result in developmental PTSD, adversely affecting children's cognitive development, speech, learning, and behaviour. 'Chronic childhood trauma interferes with the capacity to integrate sensory, emotional, and cognitive information into a cohesive whole and sets the stage for unfocused and irrelevant responses to subsequent stress' (p. 904).

The flow-on effects of cumulative traumas on children's behaviour can include delays in physical, cognitive, and emotional development, which affect their ability to take in new information and experiences and to communicate and emotionally relate to others. Streeck-Fischer and van der Kolk (2000, pp. 904–905) provide a description of a child who presented at their US clinic, to illustrate the complexity of behaviours (noting that behaviours are not generalisable amongst abused children but are shaped by their specific histories of experience):

> 8-year-old J. came for inpatient treatment following severe sexual abuse, including vaginal intercourse, beating by her father and neglect by her

mother. She displayed binge eating followed by vomiting (bulimia), food hoarding, restlessness, sudden aggressive actions, sleep disturbance with nightmares ('no, Daddy, don't do that!'), flashbacks and trance-like states, accompanied by marked general developmental retardation: physically, she appeared like a 6-year-old, but her behaviour was more like a 4-year-old. J. had lived for the last 3 years with a foster mother. She had been removed from her family by court order after her behaviour in kindergarten gave strong indication of sexual abuse and neglect. For example, she sometimes tried to sit with her genitals on her (female) teacher's face. J. frequently displayed a 'frozen' reaction in the course of everyday activity. Her face took on a mask-like expression, she moved in a jerky, tense manner, often giggling with shame, incapable of taking in anything of her surroundings. She often retreated to a small-child state, often appearing dreamy or absent, and she would suddenly cry without apparent provocation. On occasion she would become beside herself with pleasure, fall on the floor and pound her heels. Her sexualised language, her sexualised presentation of herself, her affect instability, lethargy and her avoidance of a fantasy life were pervasive.

(Streeck-Fischer and van der Kolk 2000, pp. 904–905)

The elements of this case are consistent with all four of the identified pathways to ISB as a subset of harmful sexual behaviours (Friedrich et al. 2003; Smith et al. 2019). J.'s described behaviours towards her teacher at kindergarten are consistent with ISB. The young age of onset of sexual and physical violence, her small stature and food hoarding consistent with physical neglect, the absence of loving care by both parents and her removal to foster care, as well as her traumatic stress responses disrupting her ability to relate to her current context, come together in this child's lived experiences over time. The factors contributing to harmful sexual behaviours cannot be reduced to a single formula but must be assessed as a specific history for each child, recognising that traumatic survival responses arise according to the demands of their context.

The following sections of this chapter examine some specific contexts impacting on children's vulnerabilities to expressing harmful sexual behaviours.

Victims of abuse

Exposures to sexual abuse or multiple forms of abuse are recognised risk factors for harmful sexual behaviours (Mesman et al. 2019). The abuse of children is codified in child protection laws and operationalised by statutory child protection government departments as categories of neglect, physical abuse, sexual abuse, emotional abuse, and exposure to family and domestic violence (Australian Institute of Family Studies 2018). In children's lived experience, these categories of abuse often overlap. Experiences of being neglected, physically or sexually abused, or witnessing violence against others will also be emotionally harmful (Streeck-Fischer & van der Kolk 2000). A neglectful parenting environment, or one of domestic violence or physical abuse, also raises the risks of sexual abuse by people living in the home, or by others who have contact with the children (Bromfield, Lamont, Parker, & Horsfall 2010). Preschool-aged children's exposure to persistent and intrusive sexual abuse, particularly with multiple offenders, has been found to increase the likelihood of harmful sexual behaviours in later childhood (Friedrich et al. 2003). Siblings and children in the neighbourhood, child care, or school may be affected by other children's harmful sexual behaviours and act out their experiences with others. In this way, groups of children can be affected by harmful sexual behaviours.

A review of the literature on the relationship between child sexual abuse and harmful sexual behaviours concluded that there was a significant, but not necessary, correlation:

> Sexually abused children are more likely to demonstrate problematic sexual behaviors than are non-abused children from either community settings or psychiatric settings. It is also clear, though, that many children who have been sexually abused do not develop SBP [sexual behavior problems], and likewise, many children with SBP have no known history of CSA [child sexual abuse].
> (Elkovitch, Latzman, Hansen, & Flood 2009, p. 591)

Complex trauma arising from different events of abuse over time forces victims into a continuing state of hyper-alert vigilance and survival reactions, inhibiting their ability to take in new information, recognise, and respond appropriately to social and behavioural cues in interactions with others. As in the case of J. detailed earlier (Streeck-Fischer & van der Kolk 2000, pp. 904–905), acting out problem sexual behaviours can be a learned response to the demands of sexual abusers, a copying of behaviours they have witnessed, or impulses triggered by environmental cues associated with sexual activity. For example, toileting is a common context offering opportunity for sexual abuse of infant children, and toilets are a common site of harmful sexual behaviours in care and education settings.

Family context

The primary influence on young children's development, behaviour, and learning is the home environment. Family dynamics and relationships shape social learning about how to interact with others and conventions of communication. Research has identified a number of factors in the family contexts of children who have presented with problem sexualised behaviours.

Exposure to coercive behaviours in the home environment has been identified as a risk factor for harmful sexual behaviours (Friedrich et al. 2003; Mesman et al. 2019; Silovsky & Niec 2002). Family violence behaviours such as threats, physical assaults, painful or frightening punishments, witnessing violence and abuse of other family members and pets, rejection, silencing, isolation, and humiliation provide relationship models without regard for others' feelings, needs, and interests, as well as normalising coercive interactions. Living in environments of constant danger triggers activation of trauma responses geared to survival (Streeck-Fischer & van der Kolk 2000) which become a developmental adaptation. Children living with abuse are on constant alert, with the consequence that environmental cues are filtered through stress reactions learned through past experiences. Social and behavioural cues from others are not recognised or interpreted as the child is responding with reactive survival behaviours. When children enter child care and education services, they enact known interaction dynamics.

Family practices such as public nudity, co-bathing, co-sleeping, and public sexual behaviour have also been identified as risk factors for harmful sexual behaviours (Curwen, Jenkins, & Worling 2014; Friedrich et al. 2003; Levesque, Bigras, & Pauze 2010). Family environments which expose children to nudity, witnessing adult sexual behaviours, and imagery of nudity and sexual behaviours do not establish socially expected boundaries between appropriate and inappropriate exposures of genitals and sexual behaviour. Children engaging in harmful sexual behaviours have been identified as having poor personal boundaries and understanding of social expectations of genital privacy. This also places them at risk of being sexually victimised by others (Elkovitch et al. 2009; Mesman et al. 2019). Children learn social behaviours through direct experience, guidance and instruction, and by observing and copying the behaviour of others. When behaviours in the child's household normalise coercive interactions or do not establish personal boundaries, children carry these relationship practices into care and education sites.

There is also evidence that stressed, distracted, or neglectful parenting is linked with harmful sexual behaviours (Mesman et al. 2019). Parents who are distracted from their child's exposures to environmental hazards can be unaware of the child's experiences. Such hazards could include the child's exposures to addiction behaviours such as alcohol, prescription and illicit drugs, adult abusers, children with problem sexual behaviours, and pornography. Parents who work long hours, leaving their children unsupervised or in others' informal care, are unable to monitor or control their child's experiences. Parenting behaviour can be inconsistent, and they may ignore the child, react harshly, or leave the child without reliable access to trusted, responsive support. Single-parent households were more likely to experience stress, poverty, and lack of parenting time with children (Elkovitch et al. 2009), making them more vulnerable to factors linked with harmful sexual behaviours.

Children with an intellectual disability

Children with disabilities are particularly vulnerable to all forms of child maltreatment. Briggs (2012, p. 238) identifies that children with disabilities, particularly those with high care needs, are less likely to be informed of their rights and have learned to accept being within the control of their carers, and are thus less likely to question what happens to them. Children with disabilities are often more socially isolated and therefore less able to communicate with others about abuse experiences. They may also be less able to articulate what has occurred (Briggs 2012; Evertsz & Kirsner 2003).

Children with disabilities have a greater dependence on care providers, both in the family and by external providers in care settings, making them more vulnerable to sexual predators acting in care and transport roles and to other children exhibiting problem sexual behaviours. Children with intellectual disabilities often exhibit poor impulse control and may miss out on sex education classes, or feedback on appropriate behaviour by carers (Evertsz & Kirsner, 2003).

Briggs (2012, p. 238) notes the following increased risks of exposure to abuse for children with disabilities:

- children with intellectual disabilities can be targeted by child sex offenders because police are unlikely to act if they are the sole witness;
- they often have limited social environments using special transport and few opportunities to develop normal peer relationships;
- they can become desensitised to normal adult behaviour outside institutional settings, making it difficult for them to discriminate between appropriate and inappropriate touching;
- with restricted opportunities for independence, they lack the daily problem-solving, decision-making, and confidence-building experiences available to other children;

- institutions often support adults reported for offending against children, and children have no control over their environment;
- compliance and powerlessness are fed by feelings of low self-worth, social isolation, and helplessness. This increases along with impaired communication skills. They are emotionally vulnerable to offenders' grooming methods;
- they are physically handled by more people for much longer than non-disabled children. Some are dependent on others for personal hygiene and basic care. They are assisted into taxis and special buses. Strong emotional attachments are often formed with carers. The level of vulnerability to abuse increases with the prolongation of dependency and the number of carers involved.

Incidence statistics of child abuse rely on reported events; however, it is estimated that fewer than 30% of all sexual assaults on children are reported (Stanley, Tomison, & Pocock 2003). Furthermore, children with intellectual disabilities are less likely to be able to report and, when abuse is reported, they are more likely to be ignored (Evertsz & Miller 2012; Glaser & Bentovim 1979; Royal Commission into Institutional Responses to Child Sexual Abuse 2017; Sullivan & Knutson 2000). Without identification and reporting, sexual offending against children with intellectual disabilities remains largely invisible and unchecked whilst they are further exposed to other children with problem sexual behaviours.

The risk factors for this group are perpetuated by the limits of effective responses to children with intellectual disabilities exhibiting harmful sexual behaviours. Family and professional carers require education in identifying harmful sexual behaviours and training in establishing child-safe environments to ensure that opportunities for such behaviours are limited and that incidents are reported; children receive support to learn about appropriate touching, and their rights over their body and the rights of others; and that children are able to feel safe in their day-to-day routines.

Media

Media have become increasingly sexualised across all forms of entertainment and consumption, from popular music videos on television (Ey & McInnes 2015; Wright et al. 2018) through to children's clothing (Edwards 2018). Young children consume media in their environment, including content accessed by adults and older siblings in the home, as well as in public places such as cinemas and shopping centres. Imagery of girls and young women performing sexual gestures, or dressed in clothing with brands such as 'Porn Star', or that emphasises sexualised body parts, normalises a culture of presenting girls for sexual consumption and positioning males as consumers of girls' sexual availability.

Media is not identified in the research literature as a causal factor for harmful sexual behaviours; however, the sexual saturation of consumption culture provides a narrative for sexualised social interactions. The heteronormative sexual discourse in the media also creates a level of dissonance for boys who have been exposed to sexual experiences with males, thereby further inhibiting them from disclosing their experiences (Briggs 2012). Children absorb the 'sex sells' messaging of advertisements and product placements, which provides blueprints for desirable self-presentation. Sexualised self-presentation becomes normalised such that major retail outlets stock items such as bikinis with padded bras, high heels, and make-up kits for young children (Bragg & Buckingham 2013). Whether or not parents purchase such items for their children does not constrain the influence of sexualised discourse about children on local culture.

Sexualised media content can trigger responses in children who have already been exposed to harmful sexual behaviours risk factors and reinforce such behaviour as 'normal'. The normalisation of child sexualisation also masks the potential for harm arising from harmful sexual behaviours, allowing adults to dismiss harmful sexual behaviours as harmless rehearsals of adult sex roles rather than to recognise it as inappropriate, damaging conduct which requires intervention, investigation, and safety strategies.

Pornography

The ubiquity of internet pornography and children's exposure to digital screens (televisions, smart phones, tablets, and computers) has raised the opportunities for incidental exposures to explicit sexual content arising from screen pop-ups, cyber-predators, sexual imagery circulated by sexting, and content accessed by other older users of digital screens in the child's environment (Greenfield 2004). Briggs (2012) notes the rapid growth in internet circulation of child exploitation material and ever more extreme forms of explicit sexual content, including multiple participants in sexual activity, bestiality, and extreme violence.

Flood (2009) identifies that children who are exposed to pornography have varying responses depending on their age and the context, frequency, and content of exposure. Children who are exposed to pornography acquire information about sexual activity which may variously increase their vulnerability to sexual predators, normalise violent or coercive behaviours as part of sexual expression, or shock and distress them. Children who are exposed to pornography whilst living in households with sexually abusive or violent behaviours or neglectful parenting lack information, guidance, and support about such exposures and have increased risk of harmful sexual behaviours (Smith et al. 2019). Exposure to pornography has been correlated with an increased likelihood that post-pubertal children will express attitudes and engage in behaviours depicted in pornography (Wright 2014).

Conclusion

The influences on harmful sexual behaviours of young children cannot be reduced to a simple checklist but reflect a confluence of experiences which disrupt young children's development and age-appropriate behaviour (Tucci, Mitchell & Tronick 2020). Complex trauma involving developmental post-traumatic stress disorder disrupts children's ability to engage positively with social environments, and they instead respond with survival and coping behaviours elicited by their traumatising experiences. Experiences of sexual abuse have been identified as significant, particularly if these are physically invasive, commence when the child is very young, are recurrent, and involve multiple offenders. Physical violence to the child and to other family members also raises the risk of the child's aggression towards others, including harmful sexual behaviours. Family environments of neglectful parenting and exposures to nudity and sexual behaviour by other household members, or pornography and other sexualised media content, also increase the risk of harmful sexual behaviours. Children may also act out or repeat the behaviours of other children. Children with intellectual disabilities are at particular risk as they are more likely to experience sexual abuse in care settings where they rely on personal attendants, lack cognitive and communication abilities and impulse control, and may be exposed to the harmful sexual behaviours of other children in care. Children who display harmful sexual behaviours require careful investigation and evaluation of their past experiences and home environment to identify and address the circumstances that have influenced the development of these behaviours.

References

Australian Institute of Family Studies 2018, *What is child abuse and neglect? CFCA resource sheet*, AIFS, Melbourne, viewed 14 January 2020, <https://aifs.gov.au/cfca/publications/what-child-abuse-and-neglect>.

Baker, AJL, Gries, L, Schneiderman, M, Parker, R, Archer, M & Friedrich, B 2008, 'Children with problematic sexualised behaviours in the child welfare system', *Child Welfare*, vol. 87, no. 1, pp. 5–27, viewed 14 January 2020, <http://search.proquest.com/docview/213807752?pq-origsite=gscholar>.

Bonner, BL, Walker, CE & Berliner, L 1999, *Children with sexual behavior problems: Assessment and treatment*, U.S. Department of Health and Human

Services, Administration for Children, Youth and Families, National Center on Child Abuse and Neglect, Washington, DC.

Bragg, S & Buckingham, D 2013, 'Global concerns, local negotiations and moral selves', *Feminist Media Studies*, vol. 13 no. 4, pp. 643–659, <https://doi.org/10.1080/14680777.2012.700523>.

Briggs, F 2012, *Child Protection: The essential guide for teachers and professionals whose work involves children*, Jojo Publishing, Docklands, Victoria.

Bromfield, L, Lamont, A, Parker, R & Horsfall, B 2010, *Issues for the safety & wellbeing of children in families with multiple &complex problems: The co-occurrence of domestic violence, parental substance misuse, and mental health problems*, NCPC Issues Paper 33, AIFS, Melbourne.

Chaffin, M 2008, 'Our minds are made up – don't confuse us with the facts', *Child Maltreatment*, vol. 13, no. 2, pp. 110–121.

Curwen, T, Jenkins, JM & Worling, JR 2014, 'Differentiating children with and without a history of repeated problematic sexual behavior', *Journal of Child Sexual Abuse*, vol. 23, no. 4, pp. 462–480, <https://doi.org/10.1080/10538712.2014.906529>.

Edwards, T 2018, 'Living dolls? The role of clothing and fashion in "sexualisation"', *Sexualities*, <https://doi.org/10.1177/1363460718757951>.

Elkovitch, N, Latzman, RD, Hansen, DJ & Flood, MF 2009, 'Understanding child sexual behavior problems: A developmental psychopathology framework', *Clinical Psychology Review*, vol. 29, no. 7, pp. 586–598.

Evertsz, J & Kirsner, J 2003, *Issues for intellectually disabled children with problem sexual behaviours: Literature review and research report*, Australian Childhood Foundation, Department of Human Services, Melbourne.

Evertsz, J & Miller, R 2012, *Children with problem sexual behaviours and their families: Best interests case practice model: Specialist practice resource*, Department of Human Services, Melbourne.

Ey, L & McInnes, E 2015, 'Sexualised music videos broadcast on Australian free-to-air television in child friendly time periods', *Children Australia*, vol. 40, no. 1, pp. 58–68, <https://doi.org/10.1017/cha.2014.39>.

Flood, M 2009, 'The harms of pornography exposure among children and young people', *Child Abuse Review*, vol. 8, no. 6, pp. 384–400.

Friedrich, WN 1993, 'Sexual victimization and sexual behavior in children: A review of recent literature', *Child Abuse and Neglect*, vol. 17, pp. 59–66, <https://doi.org/10.1016/0145-2134(93)90008-S>.

Friedrich, WN, Bakery, AJL, Parker, R, Schneiderman, M, Gries, L, & Archer, M 2005, 'Youth with Problematic Sexualized Behaviors in the Child Welfare System: A One-Year Longitudinal Study, *Sexual Abuse*, vol. 17, no. 4, pp. 391–406. 10.1177/107906320501700404>

Friedrich, WN, Davies, W, Feher, E & Wright, J 2003, 'Sexual behavior problems in preteen children', *Annuals of the New York Academy of Sciences*, vol. 989, no. 1, pp. 95–104, <https://doi.org/10.1111/j.1749-6632.2003.tb07296.x>.

Friedrich, W, Fisher, J, Dittner, C, Acton, R, Berliner, L, Butler, J, Damon, L, Davies, W, Gray, A & Wright, J 2001, 'Child Sexual Behavior Inventory: Normative,

Psychiatric, and Sexual Abuse Comparisons', *Child Maltreatment*, vol. 6, pp. 37–49. 10.1177/1077559501006001004

Friedrich, WN, Gully, KJ & Trane, S T 2005, 'It is a mistake to conclude that sexual abuse and sexualized behavior are not related: A reply to Drach, Wientzen, and Ricci (2001)', *Child Abuse and Neglect*, vol. 29, no. 4, pp. 297–302, <https://doi.org/10.1016/j.chiabu.2005.03.004>.

Glaser, D & Bentovim, A 1979, 'Abuse and risk to handicapped and chronically ill children', *Child Abuse and Neglect*, vol. 3, pp. 565–575.

Greenfield, PM 2004, 'Inadvertent exposure to pornography on the Internet: Implications of peer-to-peer file-sharing networks for child development and families', *Applied Developmental Psychology*, vol. 25, no. 6, pp. 741–750.

Johnson, TC 1988, 'Child perpetrators – children who molest other children: Preliminary findings', *Child Abuse and Neglect*, vol. 12, no. 2, pp. 219–229, <https://doi.org/10.1016/0145-2134(88)90030-0>.

Johnson, TC 1989, 'Female child perpetrators: Children who molest other children', *Child Abuse and Neglect*, vol. 13, no. 4, pp. 571–585, <https://doi.org/10.1016/0145-2134(89)90061-6>.

Kambouropoulos, N 2005, 'Understanding the background of children who engage in problem sexual behaviour', P Staiger (ed), *Children who engage in problem sexual behaviour: Context, characteristics and treatment*, Australian Childhood Foundation, Melbourne.

Levesque, M, Bigras, M & Pauze, R 2010, 'Externalizing problems and problematic sexual behaviors: Same etiology?' *Aggressive Behavior*, vol. 36, no. 6, pp. 358–370.

Merrick, MT, Litrownick, AJ, Everson, MD & Cox, CE 2008, 'Beyond sexual abuse: The impact of other maltreatment experiences on sexualized behaviors', *Child Maltreatment*, vol. 13, no. 2, pp. 122–132.

Mesman, GR, Harper, SL, Edge, NA, Brandt, TW & Pemberton, JL 2019, 'Problematic sexual behaviour in children', *Journal of Pediatric Health Care*, vol. 33, no. 3, pp. 323–331, <https://doi.org/10.1016/j.pedhc.2018.11.002>.

Royal Commission into Institutional Responses to Child Sexual Abuse 2017, *Final report: Preface and summary*, Commonwealth of Australia, Canberra.

Shaw, JA, Lewis, JE, Loeb, A, Rosado, J & Rodriguez, RA 2000, 'Child on child sexual abuse: Psychological perspectives', *Child Abuse and Neglect*, vol. 24, no. 12, pp. 1591–1600, <https://doi.org/10.1016/S0145-2134(00)00212-X>.

Shlonsky, A, Albers, B, Tolliday, D, Wilson, S, Norvell, J & Kissinger, L 2017, *Rapid evidence assessment: Current best evidence in the therapeutic treatment of children with problem or harmful sexual behaviours, and children who have sexually offended*, Royal Commission into Institutional Responses to Child Sexual Abuse, Commonwealth Government, Sydney, <www.childabuseroyalcommission.gov.au/policy-and-research/our-research/publishedresearch/therapeutic-treatment-of-children-with-problem-or>.

Silovsky, J & Niec, L 2002, 'Characteristics of young children with sexual behaviour problems: A pilot study', *Child Maltreatment*, vol. 7, no. 3, pp. 187–197, <https://doi.org/10.1177/1077559502007003002>.

Smith, TJ, Lindsey, RA, Bohora, S & Silovsky, JS 2019, 'Predictors of intrusive sexual behaviors in preschool-aged children', *The Journal of Sex Research*, vol. 56, no. 2, pp. 229–238, <https://doi.org/10.1080/00224499.2018.1447639>.

Sperry, DM & Gilbert, BO 2005, 'Child peer sexual abuse: Preliminary data on outcomes and disclosure experiences', *Child Abuse and Neglect*, vol. 29, no. 8, pp. 889–904, <https://doi.org/10.1016/j.chiabu.2004.12.011>.

Stanley, J, Tomison, AM & Pocock, J 2003, Child abuse and neglect in Indigenous Australian communities', *Child Abuse Prevention Issues*, no. 19, viewed 14 January 2020, <www.aifs.gov.au/nch/pubs/issues/issues19/issues19.html>.

Streeck-Fischer, A & van der Kolk, B 2000, 'Down will come baby, cradle and all: Diagnostic and therapeutic implications of chronic trauma on child development', *Australian and New Zealand Journal of Psychiatry*, vol. 34, no. 6, pp. 903–918.

Sullivan, PM & Knutson, JF 2000, 'Maltreatment and disabilities: A population-based epidemiological study', *Child Abuse and Neglect*, vol. 24, no. 10, pp. 1257–1273.

Tarren-Sweeney, M 2008, 'Predictors of problematic sexual behavior among children with complex maltreatment histories', *Child Maltreatment*, vol. 13, no. 2, pp. 182–198.

Tucci, J, Mitchell, J & Tronick, E 2020, *Handbook of therapeutic care for children*, Australian Childhood Foundation, Melbourne.

Wright, CL, Carpentier, FD, Ey, L, Hall, C, Hopper, KM & Warburton, W, 'Sexualization of popular music', *Report of the division 14 task force on the sexualization of popular music, division 46 (Society for Media Psychology & Technology) of the American Psychological Association*, American Psychological Association, US, 2018, Washington DC, <www.apadivisions.org/division-46/publications/popular-music-sexualization.pdf>.

Wright, PJ 2014, 'Pornography and the sexual socialization of children: Current knowledge and a theoretical future', *Journal of Children and Media*, vol. 8, no. 3, pp. 305–312, <https://doi.org/10.1080/17482798.2014.923606>.

6 Laws and responsibilities

Introduction

The differentiation of harmful sexual behaviours and sexual crimes involving children is one of legal distinctions on the basis of age, in turn defining the responsibilities of professionals and the processes of responses to such events. This chapter examines harmful sexual behaviour through an Australian legal lens and explains state and federal legislation relating to sexual behaviour in children under the age of 18 years. It provides a critical assessment of the ways in which the family law system intersects with child protection issues and discusses the complexities when harmful sexual behaviour is grounded in abuse within families. The chapter discusses how Australian legislation has informed school policy and practice and establishes the legal responsibility for Australian education departments, educators, and other professionals to uphold their duty of care to children.

Sexual behaviours involving children and Australian laws

In Australian law, children are defined as people aged less than 18 years. Children are not legally defined as able to consent to sexual activities before the age of at least 16 (17 in Tasmania and South Australia), regardless of whether or not they could be deemed to be willing participants (Australian Institute of Family Studies 2017a; Boxall & Fuller 2016). Sexual activities include contact behaviours such as touching and penetrative acts, as well as non-contact behaviours such as grooming and exposure to sexual acts. Except for Queensland and the Australian Capital Territory, there is a specific offence relating to persons in supervisory roles over 16- or 17-year-old children, such as teachers, foster parents, or religious leaders (Australian Institute of Family Studies 2017b).

Child sexual abuse is one of the most difficult behaviours to identify, stop, and prosecute. This is partly because Australia's legal frameworks governing sexual crimes are spread over eight jurisdictions, whilst parliamentary legislation relating to sexual conduct is enunciated across federal laws and those of five states and two territories. A key challenge of this context is ensuring the alignment and consistency of relevant statutes across the nation.

A further complexity is the structure of legal systems. Family law, which governs arrangements for children after parental separation, adjudicates on allegations of child sexual abuse by a parent when raised by state child protection services, children or the other parent during custody cases. State and territory laws define criminal conduct by adults and provide a justice system delivered through magistrates' and superior courts, whilst crimes by children and child protection orders are adjudicated in state-based youth courts. An allegation of child sexual abuse could thus come before the federal family court, a state magistrate's court, or a state youth court.

Prosecution of child sex offences is a difficult process in Australia (Cossins 2010). There is a high level of attrition between reports of offences and successful prosecution and conviction (Wundersitz 2003). A number of factors inhibit prosecution. In the first instance, identifying child sexual abuse is difficult because it is not typically visually identifiable, particularly once children are toilet-trained. Children also often delay or avoid disclosure because they may not know or be able to describe what has happened, or they may not realise it is wrong or illegal, or they may have been threatened by the offender to remain silent (Briggs 2012; Royal Commission into Institutional Responses to Child Sexual Abuse 2017b). It is difficult to obtain witness evidence from young child victims, and apart from their knowledge and language ability to speak of what has happened, courts do not commonly accept evidence from children under 7 years as they are seen as unable to comprehend the meaning of taking an oath to tell the truth. Children's accounts of their experience will often be given in court years after the events occurred and will be challenged by defence barristers (Cossins 2010; Eastwood 2003).

States and territories determine mandatory reporting laws governing who is obligated to report suspected child abuse or neglect (Australian Institute of Family Studies 2017b). The state- and territory-run child protection systems govern the handling of reports and the required responses by the government department.

States and territories also administer working with children checks for workers and volunteers and maintain registers of sex offenders, both of which interact with a national database. An Australian Child Protection Offender Reporting scheme is established by legislation in each Australian state and territory. This national scheme requires child sex offenders, and other defined categories of serious offenders against children, to keep police informed of their whereabouts and other personal details for a period of time after they are released into the community.

Under the Commonwealth Criminal Code Act 1995, the Australian Federal Police investigate online child exploitation activities. The *Passports Legislation Amendment (Overseas Travel by Child Sex Offenders) Act 2017* prevents Australians from travelling to other countries to sexually abuse children.

Australia's legal framework thus provides for reporting child sexual abuse suspicions, prosecuting child sex offenders, and for checking the criminal records of people who work or volunteer with children to prevent convicted child sex offenders from engaging in work with children. These processes proceed from a paradigm where perpetrators are adults or older children and can reasonably be held accountable for their actions. Harmful sexual behaviour by children aged under 10 is encompassed within child protection laws but outside criminal law, thus differentiating such behaviour from other sexual acts involving children.

Legal age and culpability of sexual behaviour: Australian states and territories

Harmful sexual behaviour by children aged less than 10 years cannot be treated as a crime, regardless of the degree of severity or impacts of the behaviour on children who are affected by the behaviour.

The minimum age of criminal responsibility is defined in each Australian jurisdiction as 10 years. There is a legal presumption of *doli incapax* in place for children aged between 10 and 14 years,[1] which provides for a rebuttable presumption that children in this age range cannot be legally responsible for their actions (Richards 2011). Eighteen years is the age at which a person can be treated as an adult for criminal responsibility in all Australian jurisdictions[2] (Blackley & Bartels 2018).

The legal frameworks of youth justice aim to recognise children's developmental differences and to emphasise children's potential for positive behaviour change. Youth courts exercise jurisdiction over breaches of law by young people aged 10 to 17 years, as well as child protection matters and issues of adoption and surrogacy.

The relevant legal framework for harmful sexual behaviours is the relevant child protection legislation and instruments (such as mandatory reporting requirements) wherein the behaviours are reportable by designated persons such as educators, social workers, and health professionals or the general public. Mandatory reporting ensures notification of incidents to state and territory child protection departments when the reporter identifies an event or interaction as harmful sexual behaviour. This implies that the behaviours have occurred or been identified outside private premises, such as in education sites or medical services.

Harmful sexual behaviours between young children in private residences, including family homes, are much less likely to be identified or reported. In private settings, parents have reported such observed behaviours by young children in the context of parental separation, raising concerns that sexual abuse has occurred, giving rise to young children's sexualised conduct. Sexual behaviours by children can thus also be raised under federal family law.

The problem with family law in Australia

The Australian federal family law system governs living arrangements for children after parental separation but relies on state and territory child protection systems to assess reports of child abuse. Being a civil court, the family court is not set up to make determinations of a criminal nature, such as child sexual abuse, so the system makes determinations of 'unacceptable risk of abuse' if the court is satisfied that a child is at future risk (Higgins & Kaspiew 2011; Rendell, Rathus, & Lynch 2000).

The family law system deals with prospective determinations. Unlike state- and territory-based child protection and criminal law, the decisions made under the *Family Law Act* (1975) deal with the future in deciding where a child of separated parents will live and their contact with family members (Higgins & Kaspiew 2011). Under state and territory criminal law, reports of children's experiences of sexualised conduct are examined by child protection and police investigators to determine what has happened in the past and how to respond, but the family law determinations shape a child's future and are not bound by what has happened in the past. There are many cases in which past instances of child sexual abuse have not prevented a child being ordered under Family Law to live with or have contact with the offender (McInnes 2014; McInnes 2003).

Family law decisions that place children in the care of parents who are child sex offenders expose them to continuing risk of child sexual abuse and the consequent additional risk of acting out their experiences with other children with whom they come into contact. When children are the subject of family law system orders which place the child in the care of a parent who they allege has sexually abused them, the non-offending parent is normally barred from seeking any therapeutic care for the child. This means that these children cannot have treatment or counselling if they are engaging in harmful sexual behaviour. Most children affected by harmful sexual behaviour are identified when they attend services outside the home.

Laws guiding school policies on harmful sexual behaviour

Australia's compulsory education system for children aged 5–17 provides a universal gateway bringing children into contact with education services. Educators have extensive day-to-day exposure to children outside their family home and thus have a key role in identifying indicators of child safety concerns (Briggs 2012). In all states and territories, educators, including child care providers, early childhood educators, and school teachers, are included as mandated reporters where they have a 'reasonable suspicion' or 'belief on reasonable grounds' that the child has experienced, or is at risk of, harm. New South Wales legislation specifies risk of 'significant harm' (Australian Institute of Family Studies 2017b). Queensland, Victoria, and the Australian Capital Territory only mandate reporting of physical and sexual abuse. New South Wales, Tasmania, Western Australia, and the Northern Territory's report requirements encompass physical and sexual abuse as well as emotional or psychological abuse, neglect, and exposure to domestic violence. South Australia follows this formula, except it categorises exposure to family violence as emotional abuse (Australian Institute of Family Studies 2017b). South Australian educators are mandated to report suspicion on reasonable grounds that a child or young person is, or may be, at risk. This is defined in the *Children and Young People (Safety) Act 2017* (SA).

The state and territory child protection systems have primary responsibility in managing responses to reports of harmful sexual behaviour among children. The Australian Institute of Health and Welfare maps the processes following receipt of reports of a concern of child abuse in Figure 6.1.

As Figure 6.1 indicates, reports to child protection systems are screened to determine if they reach a threshold of a child protection notification, or if they are defined as a family support matter and referred to other services. Child protection services have a responsibility to assess the needs of children and families who are the subject of mandatory reports for therapeutic services, where these are available (Evertsz & Miller 2012). Reports of harmful sexual behaviours from education sites require action by child protection services to ensure children have access to therapeutic intervention.

Aside from mandatory reporting obligations, education sites such as schools, long day care, kindergartens, and preschools have continuing responsibility to provide a safe environment for staff and children (Department for Education 2019). Harmful sexual behaviours by children attending the site have to be managed in order to stop the behaviour, re-establish safety for all children who have been affected, and ensure that families have the information they need, whilst ensuring the privacy of those involved (Department for Education and Child Development 2013). The *Young Offenders Act SA 1993* requires that the identities of children affected by harmful sexual

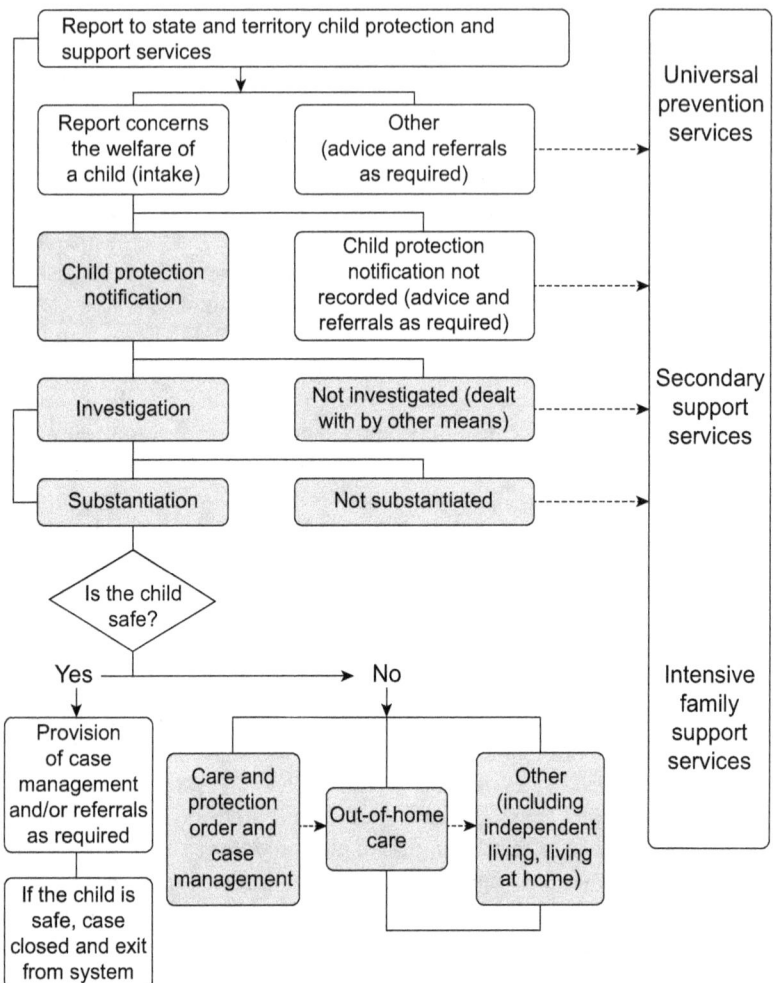

Figure 6.1 Child protection process in Australia 2017–18, AIHW 2019 (Peterson 2010)

behaviour are protected in South Australia, and similar provisions apply in other states and territories. Educators are thus on the frontline of maintaining child safety, informing directly affected families and the wider school community, whilst protecting privacy of those directly involved.

Ongoing duty of care

As represented in Figure 6.1, a mandatory report to child protection central intake lines triggers an assessment and classification guiding subsequent action. This involves investigating the concerning incident/s and communicating with the families of children who have been directly involved. The focus on children's support and recovery does not necessarily extend to investigation of potential sources of sexualisation in the lives of children who have initiated problematic sexual activities. This is contrary to research, which has identified child sexual abuse, including exposure to explicit sexual material, as a precursor factor to most cases of harmful sexual behaviours by children (Hackett 2011; Shlonsky et al. 2017). When child protection investigations of family contexts are conducted, police may or may not be involved, with a consequence that children may receive therapy to stop the behaviours, whilst continuing to live with a family context where they are exposed to abuse. This contingency means that therapeutic intervention for children can be undermined by an absence of safety.

For privacy reasons, educators are not typically directly informed by child protection services of the outcomes for children who have been the subject of a mandatory report to child protection services. The child protection agencies' actions subsequent to the mandatory report may result in no apparent changes to a child's context. The child's access to therapeutic support, the family's role in relation to the child's recovery, and ongoing action is unlikely to be actively discussed with staff who made the report (McCallum 2000). Education staff have an ongoing duty of care to manage safety of children and peer relationships without direct information or control over children's circumstances or their access to effective therapeutic intervention.

Conclusion

Australia has a complex legal framework pertaining to sexual activity involving young children which is primarily aimed at protecting children from older or adult offenders. Beyond mandatory reporting, the legal obligations arising from harmful sexual behaviours among young children aged less than 10 years are not prescribed. There is an expectation that children involved in harmful sexual behaviours will have access to therapeutic intervention; however, there is no guarantee that appropriate expert services will be available across Australia, including rural and remote centres.

Investigation of children's exposures to risk factors, such as exposure to sexual abuse and other forms of abuse, is not mandated and is vulnerable to resource pressures arising from the high demands in child protection systems. Cases can be closed without active investigation if there are no available staff.

The interests of children and families point to the need to ensure that children's living circumstances do not expose them to abuse. Children and families must have access to the therapeutic services they need to prevent further harmful sexual behaviour and to recover from their experiences.

Notes

1 *Crimes Act 1914* (Cth) ss 4M, 4N; *Criminal Code Act 1995* (Cth) ss 7.1, 7.2; *Criminal Code 2002* (ACT) ss 25, 26; *Children (Criminal Proceedings) Act 1987* (NSW) s 5; *Criminal Code Act 1983* (NT) ss 38(1)–(2); *Criminal Code Act 1899* (Qld) ss 29(1)–(2); *Young Offenders Act 1993* (SA) s 5; *Criminal Code Act 1924* (Tas) ss 18(1)–(2); *Children, Youth and Families Act 2005* (Vic) s 344; *Criminal Code Act Compilation Act 1913* (WA) s 29.
2 *Children and Young People Act 2008* (ACT) ss 8, 69; *Children (Criminal Proceedings) Act 1987* (NSW) s 3; *Children, Youth and Families Act 2005* (Vic) sch 3; *Youth Justice Act 2005* (NT) s 6; *Youth Justice and Other Legislation (Inclusion of 17-year-old Persons) Amendment Act 2016* (Qld); *Young Offenders Act 1993* (SA) s 4; *Youth Justice Act 1997* (Tas) s 3; *Young Offenders Act 1994* (WA) s 3.

References

Australian Institute of Family Studies (AIFS) 2017a, 'Age of consent laws', *Child, family, community Australia resource sheet*, AIFS, Melbourne, Last modified July 2017, viewed 16 May 2019, <https://aifs.gov.au/cfca/publications/age-consent-laws>.

Australian Institute of Family Studies (AIFS) 2017b, 'Mandatory reporting of child abuse and neglect', *Child, family, community Australia resource sheet*, AIFS, Melbourne, viewed 20 December 2017, <https://aifs.gov.au/cfca/publications/mandatory-reporting-child-abuse-and-neglect>

Australian Institute of Health and Welfare 2019, *Child Protection Australia 2017–2018*. AIHW, Canberra.

Blackley, R & Bartels, L 2018, 'Sentencing and treatment of juvenile sex offenders in Australia', *Trends & Issues in Crime and Criminal Justice*, no. 555, Australian Institute of Criminology, Canberra, viewed 14 January 2020, <https://aic.gov.au/publications/tandi/tandi555>.

Boxall, H & Fuller, G 2016, 'Brief review of contemporary sexual offence and child sexual abuse legislation in Australia: 2015 update', *Special report prepared for the Royal Commission into Institutional Responses to Child Sexual Abuse*, Australian Institute of Criminology, Canberra.

Briggs, F 2012, *Child Protection: The essential guide for teachers and other professionals whose work involves children*, Jojo Publishing, Docklands, Victoria.

Cossins, A 2010, *Alternative models for prosecuting child sex offences in Australia: Report of the National Child Sexual Assault Reform Committee*, School of Law UNSW, Sydney.

Department for Education 2019, *Protective practices for staff in their interactions with children and young people: Guidelines for staff working or volunteering in education and care settings*, 2nd edn, Department for Education, South Australia.

Department for Education and Child Development 2013, *Responding to problem sexual behaviour in children and young people: Guidelines for staff in education and care settings*, Department for Education and Child Development, Catholic Education South Australia, Association of Independent Schools of South Australia, Adelaide.

Eastwood, C 2003, *The experiences of child complainants of sexual abuse in the criminal justice system*, Trends & issues in crime and criminal justice no. 250, Australian Institute of Criminology, Canberra, <https://aic.gov.au/publications/tandi/tandi250>.

Evertsz, J & Miller, R 2012, *Children with problem sexual behaviour and their families*, Victorian Department of Human Services, Melbourne.

Hackett, S 2011, 'Children and young people with harmful sexual behaviors', in C Barter and D Berridge (eds), *Children behaving badly? Peer violence between children and young people*, John Wiley & Sons, Chichester, pp. 121–135.

Higgins, D & Kaspiew, R 2011, *Child protection and family law, joining the dots*, National Child Protection Clearinghouse Issues Paper Number 34, AIFS, Melbourne.

McCallum, F 2000, *The effectiveness of training as professional development: Teachers as mandated notifiers of child abuse and neglect*, University of South Australia Thesis Collection, Adelaide.

McInnes, E 2003, 'Parental alienation syndrome: A paradigm for child abuse', in *Child sexual abuse: Justice response or alternative resolution conference*, Australian Institute of Criminology, Adelaide.

McInnes, E 2014, 'Madness in family law: Mothers' mental health in the Australian family law system', *Psychiatry, psychology and law*, vol. 21, no. 1, pp. 78–91, <https://doi.org/10.1080/13218719.2013.774688>.

Peterson, C 2010, *Looking forward through the lifespan: Developmental psychology*, 5th edn, Pearson Australia, Frenchs Forest.

Rendell, K, Rathus, Z & Lynch, A 2000, *An unacceptable risk: A report on child contact arrangements where there is violence in the family*, Women's Legal Service, Brisbane.

Richards, K 2011, 'What makes juvenile offenders different from adult offenders?', *Trends & issues in crime and criminal justice*, no. 409, Australian Institute of Criminology, Canberra, viewed 14 January 2020, <https://aic.gov.au/publications/tandi/tandi409>.

Royal Commission into Institutional Responses to Child Sexual Abuse (RCIRCSA) 2017b, *Identifying and disclosing child sexual abuse: Volume 4*, Royal Commission into Institutional Responses to Child Sexual Abuse, Sydney.

Shlonsky, A, Albers, B, Tolliday, D, Wilson, S, Norvell, J & Kissinger, L 2017, *Rapid evidence assessment: Current best evidence in the therapeutic treatment of children with problem or harmful sexual behaviours, and children who have sexually offended*, Royal Commission into Institutional Responses to Child Sexual Abuse, Sydney.

Wundersitz, J 2003, 'Child victims of sexual offences: Tracking from police incident report to finalisation in Court', in *Child sexual abuse: Justice response or alternative resolution conference*, Australian Institute of Criminology, Adelaide.

7 Educator knowledge of harmful sexual behaviour and their training needs

Introduction

This chapter builds on previous chapters by presenting findings from a small-scale Australian national study that explored preschool, primary school, and out-of-school hours care educators' understanding of typical and harmful sexual behaviour. Current training specific to children's harmful sexual behaviour for educators is hard to establish because there are no known stand-alone training modules for educators in Australia. Nevertheless, this chapter reviews current state and territory guidelines alongside a research-informed understanding of what supports educators would like to supportively manage children's harmful sexual behaviour. This chapter concludes by proposing a move towards a national approach.

Educators' role in a universal education system means that they are the profession most likely to observe harmful sexual behaviours (Briggs 2012). Whilst health and family support services do have time with individual children, organised around specific tasks or programs, unlike educators they are less likely to have the time or opportunity with children to expose such behaviours. It is therefore critical that educators are equipped with the requisite knowledge and understanding of harmful sexual behaviours (Ey, McInnes, & Rigney 2017).

In 2016, 107 educators from primary schools, preschools, and out-of-school hours care services around Australia answered an online survey about their experiences involving children's displays of harmful sexual behaviours (HSB) in education settings. The survey explored how they defined such behaviours, the training and education they had received on the topic, and the kinds of training and support they would like to have to deal with this issue. Educators were recruited from all states and territories.

The research was conducted following a year in which Australian police data showed that 21 percent of legal actions for sexual offences involved children aged 10 to 17 years (Royal Commission into Institutional Responses to Child Sexual Abuse 2017c, p. 28). Of the survivors of sexual abuse who gave evidence to Australia's Royal Commission into Institutional Responses to Child Sexual Abuse, more than 23% said their experience involved another child (Royal Commission into Institutional Responses to Child Sexual Abuse 2017c). The experience of unwanted sexual behaviours at a young age had enduring impacts (Friedrich 1993) even though another child, and not an adult, was involved.

The findings from the recent Royal Commission into Institutional Responses to Child Sexual Abuse (2017c) and the South Australian Child Protection Systems Royal Commission (Nyland 2016) identify two key issues:

> (a) children and their parents are less disposed to accept sexual harassment as a normal part of growing up and are legally challenging these claims outside of school, and (b) there is a need for more education to assist practitioners working with children and young people and their families to deal specifically with issues relating to problematic sexual behaviours.
>
> (Ey et al. 2017, p. 682)

Educators' understanding of developmentally normal and harmful sexual behaviour

Peer sexual assault and teachers' ability to address such harmful sexual behaviours at school pose a significant challenge to families, schools, teachers, and government policy (Finkelhor & Dziuba-Leatherman 1995; Walsh et al. 2013).

Educator training programmes on child protection in Australia are limited and conventionally delivered through courses focusing on mandated reporting of child abuse to child protection authorities (Walsh & Farrell 2008). The compulsory training in their legal obligations to report suspected child abuse (Australian Institute of Family Studies 2017) addresses a key element of teacher responsibilities; however, it is important to also skill educators in appropriate intervention strategies and ongoing trauma-informed pedagogy (Australian Childhood Foundation 2010). It is equally important that educators are able to recognise and understand why children may engage in harmful sexual behaviours.

The paradigm of victim and perpetrator invoked in mandatory reporting training for educators constructs children as the victim and older people, typically adults, as offenders. This approach reflects socio-cultural norms in relation to perceptions of child sexual abuse victims and offenders as involving people of post-pubertal ages. This paradigm thus fails to equip educators and carers to respond appropriately to situations involving harmful sexual behaviour between preschool- and primary school-aged children. Wunsch and Moran (2018) also highlight the need for teachers to receive education in how to teach protective behaviours for young children. Further problems arise where child protection training varies in scope, quality, and consistency. Some state and territory interventions are aimed at the teacher identification of abuse whilst others endeavour to promote harm minimisation (Walsh, Zwi, Woolfenden, & Shlonsky 2015).

Educators' views of typical sexual behaviour of children with whom they are currently working

Of the 71 survey participants who provided their views on children's typical sexual behaviour, the majority (92%, n = 65) were able to identify some elements of typical sexual behaviour for the children with whom they were working. One participant stated 'different things at different ages', and another stated that they were 'not sure'. One participant indicated that Year One children with whom she worked were 'not sexual'. Three referred to child protection training materials, such as the 'traffic lights' resource, that they would use to determine normal sexual behaviour for each age group. The 'traffic lights' resource is formally titled *Sexual behaviours in children and young people*. It is a guide to assist educators to identify typical and harmful sexual behaviours in children aged 0–17 years and respond appropriately (True Relationships & Reproductive Health 2015).

Forty-three participants described what they saw as typical sexual behaviour in the age groups they worked with. Those who worked with younger children identified the following:

> Normal sexual curiosity, such as curiosity about where babies come from, curiosity about body parts, and particular differences between the sexes and self-exploration. They also identified experimenting with gender roles such as playing mums and dads. Some teachers noted that as children first begin to play in gender-segregated groups, children typically expressed aversion towards the opposite sex.
> (Ey et al. 2017, p. 689)

Participants who worked with older children noted 'children demonstrating discomfort or embarrassment and/or giggling when talking about general sex or sexual information, such as sexual reproductive organs, whilst others identified discussions about sex without reference to emotional expression. Telling rude jokes and using scatological language was also acknowledged' (Ey et al. 2017, p. 689).

These participants acknowledged that older children showed signs of exploring relationships and sexual attraction, through behaviours such as flirting and an interest in affection generally. These could be demonstrated through behaviours such as kissing and holding hands. 'Two participants described behaviours such as sexual attraction, emotional crushes, and subtle flirting being typical for teenagers' (Ey et al. 2017, p. 689). The views from these two participants may be considered conservative as children commonly develop these behaviours at around the age of 10 years (Worthman, Plotsky, Schechter, & Cummings 2010).

The study revealed a tendency in participants to avoid using correct terminology for sexual reproductive organs: 'Forty-two per cent (n = 18) of respondents used the terminology "private parts", rather than labelling sexual reproduction organs as recommended in sexual education and child protection for educators' (Ey et al. 2017, p. 689).

In summary, most educators were able to identify typically developing sexual behaviour but preferred to use general euphemisms for sexual reproductive organs in their own expression. This reflects a level of discomfort for educators and suggests a need for more practice in using correct anatomical terms in order to model this with students and their families.

Educators' views of harmful sexual behaviour of children with whom they are currently working

Of the 71 respondents giving a definition of harmful sexual behaviours, the majority (93%) were able to identify some elements of harmful sexual behaviour. Amongst children aged 5–14 years, participants noted the most common behaviours they considered problematic:

> Touching others in sexual ways; simulating sexual intercourse; sexual play; secrecy, such as hiding and telling others not to tell; children having sexual knowledge beyond their age; children having an excessive interest in sexual acts; and children demonstrating sexually harassing behaviours such as inviting, coercing, luring, or forcing others to engage in sexual conduct. One participant reported that a Year Four male student had threatened to rape other students.
> (Ey et al. 2017, p. 690)

In relation to children in middle and upper primary school, participants reported frequent masturbation; viewing and discussing re-enactment of pornography; seeking sexual attention from teachers/adults or much older students; engaging in sexual acts, including oral sex and sexual actions of an explicit nature; rubbing their body against others in a sexual manner;

using explicit sexual language; engaging in sexting; and having love bites (Ey et al. 2017, p. 690).

Some educators (17%, n = 12) misidentified certain behaviours as harmful when they are in fact considered typical sexual behaviours for the age group, according to Briggs (2012). These included:

> Exposure of genitals, self-stimulation, sexually suggestive dancing and listening to songs with sexual content, using sexual innuendo, flirting, and kissing. One educator identified homophobia as a problematic sexual behaviour, which is a problematic attitude rather than a behaviour. Two educators answered that they had not seen any problematic sexual behaviours in their settings and thus did not list any behaviours. One educator stated that they were not sure which sexual behaviours were identified as problematic.
>
> (Ey et al. 2017, p. 690)

The data indicate that educators are generally able to identify sexualised behaviours of concern and differentiate these from age-typical sexual behaviours which did not infringe on others' safety and wellbeing.

Current training for educators

In the Australian Capital Territory, Queensland, and Victoria, teachers are only mandated to report sexual and physical abuse. In Western Australia, they are only mandated to report sexual abuse. In South Australia they are mandated to report physical, emotional/psychological, and sexual abuse and neglect, and in New South Wales, Tasmania, and the Northern Territory they are mandated to report physical, emotional/psychological, and sexual abuse, neglect, and exposure to domestic violence (Bromfield & Higgins 2005; Walsh, Rassafiani, Mathews, Farrell, & Butler 2010). This disparate approach to mandated notification across states and territories is problematic for effective sexual abuse prevention. Although all educators nationally are required to report sexual abuse, terms such as 'sexual abuse', 'sexual offences', 'sexual perpetrators', and 'sexual offenders' typically reference adults rather than children (Staiger et al. 2005), which may result in children's harmful sexual behaviour being overlooked (Ey et al. 2017, p. 687).

> The content in mandated notification courses on offer is not accessible to the general public and the only course empirically tested and published is the South Australian mandated notification course (Walsh & Farrell 2008), now known as *Responding to Abuse and Neglect: Education and Care*. Further research to compare and contrast state and

territory mandated notification courses is needed to ascertain what training educators receive about child protection, and more specifically, whether and how these courses address children's harmful sexual behaviours. When the complexities of harmful sexual behaviour are overlooked or misunderstood, it is difficult to identify children who may be victims of sexual abuse by adults.

(Ey et al. 2017, p. 686)

Peer-on-peer aggressive conduct in education and care sites is often construed as bullying or as children having poorly developed social skills. It attracts interventions such as physical separation, mediation between parties, or a range of school-based disciplinary strategies such as detention or exclusion (Barter & Berridge 2011). Educators and carers recognise elements of sexual behaviour as part of normal development, such as kissing, holding hands, and cuddling. Although it is well recognised that sexual development and sexual expression begins in childhood, ideas of when it is acceptable for children to engage in sexual activity are grounded in social and cultural values that change over time. Concerns arise if there is evidence of aggression or coercion by children pursuing or harassing other children, penetrative behaviours, or public exposure of genitals (Ey & McInnes 2018). A rising number of reports over the previous decade have identified preschool and junior primary school children involved in HSB in education settings (Briggs 2012; Bromfield, Hirte, Octoman, & Katz 2017, Debelle 2013; Ey & McInnes 2018). This highlights an increasing need for new understandings and responses by educators and carers to affected children and their families.

Most states and territories have produced policies and guidelines for teachers. The following section identifies those available online. The New South Wales Department of Education provides a *Child protection policy: Responding to and reporting students at risk of harm*. This outlines the 'roles and responsibilities of staff in relation to child protection including training, reporting on safety, and supporting children and young people, as well as monitoring, evaluation and reporting requirements' (NSW Department of Education 2018).

South Australia's Education Department document *Responding to problem sexual behaviour in children and young people: Guidelines for staff in education and care settings*, defines and discusses age-appropriate and harmful sexual behaviour with guidelines for staff. These relate to (a) determining the seriousness of the behaviour; (b) immediate responses by the staff member and leadership of the education setting; (c) long-term responses, including safety and support plans; and (d) a list of support services for staff, children, and their families (Department for Education 2019).

In the Northern Territory the education department has *Guidelines: Sexual behaviour in children*, giving information similar to that provided in South Australia (Department of Education: Northern Territory Government 2015). *Identifying and responding to student sexual offending* is the Victorian document which defines harmful sexual behaviours for children under 10 years and offending behaviour including sexual assault, rape, and indecent acts for children over age 10. It does not define age-appropriate behaviour. The document provides guidelines on immediate responses along with instructions to develop a support plan for those involved but does not provide a template like the Northern Territory or South Australia. There is also a list of support services (Victoria State Government Education and Training 2016). Tasmania's Department of Education provides the True Relationships and Reproductive Health's *Sexual behaviours in children and young people* guide to educators to identify, understand, and respond to sexual behaviours. The document *Transforming trauma discussion paper 3: Problem sexualised behaviour* (Australian Childhood Foundation and Tasmania Department of Education, 2012) (a) defines problem sexual behaviour and addresses concerns with how sexual behaviour is labelled; (b) defines and explains normal, concerning, and harmful sexual behaviour; (c) presents causes of harmful sexual behaviour; (d) provides guidelines for assessing problem sexual behaviour and (e) responding to problem sexual behaviour; (f) poses questions for consideration about understanding and managing problem sexual behaviour; and (h) provides references for further reading. Tasmania also conducts a workshop for educators on transforming problem sexual behaviour.

The Australian Capital Territory Education Directorate has training for primary school teachers on identifying and responding to problematic sexualised behaviours. There are policy guidelines and a training module for high schools. The focus is on addressing coercive and violent behaviours and intimate partner violence.

Queensland's guidelines are only available to staff working in education in the state. The Queensland Department of Education gives information for educators in its *Student protection guidelines* (Department of Education Queensland 2020). This is informed by True Relationships and Reproductive Health's *Sexual behaviours in children and young people* (2015). The Western Australian Education Department gives no public information about their policy documents (Ey et al. 2017, p. 686).

There are inconsistent approaches around Australia to mandatory reporting training and guidelines in identifying and responding to children's harmful sexual behaviour. This highlights a need for educators' access to consistent and holistic teacher training materials and support (Ey et al. 2017, p. 687).

Educators' training in identifying and responding to children displaying sexual behaviour

Most of the 2016 survey respondents were able to identify more than one source of training relating to harmful sexual behaviour. Sources included external agencies, teacher training, training within another discipline, and researching the topic (Ey et al. 2017).

Ey et al. (2017) report that more than half of respondents had been trained in identifying and responding to harmful sexual behaviour in children. Sixty-six of 101 participants (65.3%) indicated they had been trained. Four in every five who had been trained had done mandated reporting courses. The rest had received professional development. One in five of these had completed pre-service training at university. Ey, McInnes, and Rigney note that 26 respondents had either sought courses, read books, or searched the internet or sought information through other means (Ey et al. 2017, p. 690).

Nearly 80% of those who had received some education said it made them 'confident' in identifying and responding to children's harmful sexual behaviour. Nine out of ten respondents wanted specific courses for educators in identifying harmful sexual behaviours (Ey et al. 2017, p. 691).

What educators want

The survey identified that educators wanted on-demand access to training and expert support. Whilst all state and territory education departments provided some level of support, services were often thinly spread, and issues of child sexual behaviour did not have any priority over other issues. This meant that educators could wait for weeks before they or the children could access counselling support. A particular priority was support for educators in responding to involved families. Educators also wanted to be able to refer families to services in the wider community and have whole-of-school leadership engaged in safe behaviours education. Respondents noted that support was most effective when they could access information and guidance as needed (McInnes & Ey 2019).

Educators experienced high levels of stress when confronted with harmful sexual behaviours and wanted to be effective in protecting and supporting children. Responses from site leadership were critical for educators who needed to comply with legal frameworks, manage the learning and care needs of the children, care for their own health and wellbeing, and manage the needs of families. Respondents felt that they experienced little support when they reported harmful sexual behaviours and were not informed or aware of any action by child protection services. Principals and managers who did not act promptly or appropriately on reports of concerning behaviour were seen as failing to prevent escalating behaviours by children. Male educators felt particularly vulnerable responding to harmful sexual behaviours. Educators were highly vulnerable to vicarious trauma, toxic stress, and burnout, owing to the combination of being exposed to harmful sexual behaviours, limited or delayed support from school leadership and counselling and therapeutic services, ongoing impacts on children's behaviour in their classroom environment, and the ongoing concerns of families (McInnes & Ey 2019).

The psychological and emotional impacts on educators of being exposed to harmful sexual behaviours are currently largely unacknowledged in formal, systemic responses. Such impacts include the responsibility to maintain the safety of all students, legal obligations to make mandatory reports, managing learning in ways which take account of children's trauma histories, and liaising with families whose children have been directly and indirectly involved. A consequent risk of harmful sexual behaviours, apart from impacts on children and families, is the impact on the learning environment and the wellbeing of educators.

A move to a national approach

The survey findings highlighted the need for harmful sexual behaviours to be included as a specific issue in pre-service teacher training programs in universities, in child protective behaviours curricula, and in mandatory training in responding to child abuse and neglect. Developing a national approach to harmful sexual behaviours training for educators would enable the development of a shared language, definitions, reporting and response frameworks, and pedagogy approaches.

Several strategies are indicated as critical to ensuring that the harms caused by harmful sexual behaviours can be prevented and reduced. These include multiple forms of access to information and training for educators in identifying and responding to harmful sexual behaviours, greater access to counselling and therapeutic services for affected children, and expert and continuing support in managing family needs. Feedback to educators on actions by child protection services is important for enabling educators to form part of a team approach to support children's safety and recovery.

The social problems of domestic violence, parental substance abuse, and child abuse inform children's social learnings, which manifest in their behaviour in education sites. Educators are on the front line of identifying harmful sexual behaviours and providing effective response to prevent ongoing and future harms. More training, more services, and more support need to be focused on harmful sexual behaviours to improve outcomes.

Conclusion

Educators bear the brunt of responsibility in identifying, reporting, responding to, and managing harmful sexual behaviours in care and education settings. However, the research indicates that many struggle with the ongoing work of dealing with children's behaviours, parents' concerns, legal and professional obligations, and their own levels of stress. Male educators indicated their need for particular support in an environment of heightened awareness of sexual behaviours and public sensitivities to males as potential perpetrators of child sexual abuse. Both male and female educators expressed the need for priority expert attention to harmful sexual behaviours incidents in care and education sites, as these had the potential to escalate rapidly to affect multiple children. Children initiating harmful sexual behaviours required quick access to therapeutic interventions, whilst children who were directly involved in harmful sexual behaviours by other children, as well as those who witnessed or heard about the behaviour, required rapid support to deal with what occurred. Families also required multiple-level responses to be assured of the re-establishment of safety for their children in the education setting, communication and privacy needs, and ongoing access to appropriate services to assist them to deal with any emergent consequences of exposure to harmful sexual behaviours. In addition to teacher education and training, on-demand resources and support are critical to ensuring educators are not left with all the responsibility and insufficient care. This will help ensure they can meet their obligations in each circumstance.

References

Australian Childhood Foundation 2010, *Making space for learning: Trauma informed practice in schools*, Australian Childhood Foundation, Richmond, Victoria, viewed 20 January 2019, <www.childhood.org.au/for-professionals/resources>.

Australian Childhood Foundation and Tasmania Department of Education, 2012, *Transforming Trauma Project Showcase*, Department of Education, Hobart, Tasmania.

Australian Institute of Family Studies 2017b, *Mandatory reporting of child abuse and neglect*, viewed 14 January 2020, <https://aifs.gov.au/cfca/publications/mandatory-reporting-child-abuse-and-neglect>.

Barter, C & Berridge, D 2011, 'Introduction', in CBD Berridge (ed), *Children behaving badly? Peer violence between children and young people*, John Wiley & Sons Ltd, Chichester, pp. 1–18.

Briggs, F 2012, *Child protection: The essential guide for teachers and other professionals whose work involves children*, Jojo Publishing, Docklands, Victoria.

Bromfield, L & Higgins, D 2005, *National comparisons of child protection systems*, <www.aifs.gov.au/nch/pubs/issues/issues22/issues22.html>.

Bromfield, L, Hirte, C, Octoman, O & Katz, I 2017, *Child sexual abuse in Australian institutional contexts 2008–2013: Findings from administrative data*, Sydney, <www.childabuseroyalcommission.gov.au/sites/default/files/file-list/research_report_-_child_sexual_abuse_in_australian_institutional_contexts_2008-13_findings_from_administrative_data_-_causes.pdf>.

Debelle, B 2013, *South Australia Royal Commission 2012–2013: Report of independent education inquiry (edited version)*, Adelaide, <www.saasso.asn.au/wp-content/uploads/2013/11/DebelleInquiry.pdf>.

Department for Education 2019, *Responding to problem sexual behaviour in children and young people: Guidelines for staff in education and care settings*, 3rd edn, Government of South Australia: Department for Education, Adelaide, <www.education.sa.gov.au/sites/default/files/responding_to_problem_sexual_behaviour_in_children_and_young_people.pdf>.

Department of Education Queensland 2020, *Student protection guidelines*, Department of Education Queensland. <http://ppr.det.qld.gov.au/education/community/Procedure%20Attachments/Student%20Protection/student-protection.pdf>

Department of Education: Northern Territory Government 2015, *Guidelines: Sexual behaviour in children*, Department of Education: Northern Territory Government, Perth, <https://education.nt.gov.au/__data/assets/pdf_file/0006/258108/Sexual-behaviour-in-children-guidelines.pdf>.

Ey, L, McInnes, E & Rigney, L 2017, 'Educators' understanding of young children's typical and problematic sexual behaviour and their training in this area', *Sex education*, vol. 17, no. 6, pp. 682–696, <https://doi.org/10.1080/14681811.2017.1357030>.

Ey, L, & McInnes, E 2018, 'Educators' Observations of Children's Display of Problematic Sexual Behaviors in Educational Settings,' *Journal of Child Sexual Abuse*, vol. 27, no. 1, pp. 88–105, doi: 10.1080/10538712.2017.1349855.

Finkelhor, D & Dziuba-Leatherman, J 1995, 'Victimization prevention programs: A national survey of children's exposure and reactions', *Child Abuse and Neglect*, vol. 19, no. 2, pp. 129–139.

Friedrich, WN 1993, 'Sexual victimization and sexual behavior in children: A review of recent literature', *Child Abuse and Neglect*, vol. 17, no. 1, pp. 59–66, <https://doi.org/10.1016/0145-2134(93)90008-S>.

McInnes, E & Ey, L 2019, Responding to problematic sexual behaviours of primary school children: Supporting care and education staff, *Sex Education*, vol. 20, no. 1, pp. 75–89, <https://doi.org/10.1080/14681811.2019.1621827>.

New South Wales Department of Education 2018, *Child protection policy: Responding to and reporting students at risk of harm*, Department of Education,

Sydney, viewed 17 December 2019, <https://education.nsw.gov.au/policy-library/policies/child-protection-policy-responding-to-and-reporting-students-at-risk-of-harm>.

Nyland, M 2016, *The life they deserve: Child protection systems royal commission report*, South Australia, viewed 13 January 2020, <https://agdsa.govcms.gov.au/sites/default/files/complete_report_child_protection_systems_royal_commission_report.pdf?acsf_files_redirect>.

Royal Commission into Institutional Responses to Child Sexual Abuse, 2017c, *Final report: Volume 10, children with harmful sexual behaviours*, Sydney, <www.childabuseroyalcommission.gov.au/sites/default/files/final_report_-_volume_10_children_with_harmful_sexual_behaviours.pdf>.

Staiger, P 2005, *Children who engage in problem sexual behaviours: Context, characteristics and treatment; A review of the literature*, Australian Childhood Foundation and Deakin University, Melbourne.

True Relationships and Reproductive Health 2015, *Sexual behaviours in children and young people*, True Relationships and Reproductive Health, Windsor, Queensland.

Victoria State Government Education and Training 2016, *Identifying and responding to student sexual offending*, Victoria State Government, Melbourne.

Walsh, K & Farrell, A 2008, 'Identifying and evaluating teachers' knowledge in relation to child abuse and neglect: A qualitative study with Australian early childhood teachers', *Teaching and Teacher Education*, vol. 24, no. 3, pp. 585–600, <https://doi.org/10.1016/j.tate.2007.07.003>.

Walsh, K, Mathews, B, Rassafiani, M, Farrell, A & Butler, D 2013, 'Elementary teachers' knowledge of legislative and policy duties for reporting child sexual abuse,' *Elementary School Journal*, vol. 114, no.2, pp. 178–199.

Walsh, K, Rassafiani, M, Mathews, B, Farrell, A & Butler, D 2010, 'Teachers' attitudes toward reporting child sexual abuse: Problems with existing research leading to new scale development', *Journal of Child Sexual Abuse*, vol. 19, no. 3, pp. 310–336, <https://doi.org/10.1080/10538711003781392>.

Walsh, K, Zwi, K, Woolfenden, S & Shlonsky, A 2015, 'School-based education programmes for the prevention of child sexual abuse', *The Cochrane Library*, vol. 4, pp. 1–121, <https://doi.org/10.1002/14651858.CD004380.pub3>.

Worthman, CM, Plotsky, PM, Schechter, DS & Cummings, CA (eds) 2010, *Formative experiences: The interaction of caregiving, culture, and developmental psychology*, Cambridge University Press, New York.

Wunsch, A & Moran, C 2018, 'Traffic lights: Understanding healthy sexual development and protecting children from harm', *Educating Young Children: Learning and Teaching in the Early Childhood Years*, vol. 24, no. 3, pp. 24–26.

8 Responding to and supporting children who display harmful sexual behaviour

An educator's approach

Introduction

Chapter 8 discusses recommended practice of how to support and respond to children who display harmful sexual behaviour and those who have been affected, whilst drawing on current practices and guidelines designed to protect and support the children involved. The final focus of this chapter is on supporting children within an educational context, placing the child and their education and development at the forefront, rather than focusing only on the behaviour. Some practical ideas are deliberated.

In Australia, there are 281,948 full-time teaching staff (Australian Bureau of Statistics 2018) who, as mandated notifiers (Australian Institute of Family Studies 2017b), need to be able to recognise and respond appropriately to children's harmful sexual behaviour (HSB) in education settings to minimise ongoing social and economic impacts. Schools are increasingly charged with the responsibility of addressing complex social problems faced by children and adolescents (Skovdal & Campbell 2015) and have a responsibility to support the safety and wellbeing of all children in their care (Ministerial Council on Education: Early Childhood Development and Youth Affairs 2011). Teachers spend more time with school-age children than any other adults, other than children's parents (Briggs 2012), and play a significant role in the safety, wellbeing, and education of children. This places teachers at the forefront of those required to identify, respond to, and seek support for children with HSB and those affected by it. In Australia, teachers across all states and territories are mandated to report sexual abuse (Australian Institute of Family Studies 2017b) and are the second-largest group to report child abuse and neglect (19%), marginally below police (21%) (Australian Institute of Family Studies 2017a). However, navigating this complex and sensitive area can be difficult. Because a teacher's response to harmful sexual behaviour could significantly affect the subsequent health and development of the children involved, including children's potential contact with the judicial system, it is important that teachers respond to children in an appropriate and supportive manner.

Therapeutic treatment for children who display harmful sexual behaviour

The prevalence of children's harmful sexual behaviour in Australia has resulted in a rise in the number of children attending treatment programs (Royal Commission into Institutional Responses to Child Sexual Abuse 2016). There is significant variation in the interventions offered for children with harmful sexual behaviour across Australia (Royal Commission into Institutional Responses to Child Sexual Abuse 2017b) and limited evidence for the effectiveness of these programs. This can be due to practical issues, such as children who did not complete the treatment or continue participating in the research, and a lack of research with children with harmful sexual behaviours who are not enrolled in programs (Shlonsky et al. 2017). Nevertheless, *multisystemic therapy* has been identified as a promising approach (Shlonsky et al. 2017). It is an intensive program underpinned by a range of cognitive behaviour therapies and pragmatic family therapy approaches delivered in the child's home and facilitated by the child's parent/caregiver. Multisystemic therapy interventions follow an 'ecological' model and 'are tailored to the child's individual, family, friendship, school and community environments' (Royal Commission into Institutional Responses to Child Sexual Abuse 2017b). The involvement of children's social systems is designed to uphold and maintain behaviour change (Royal Commission into Institutional Responses to Child Sexual Abuse 2017b). Multisystemic therapy's collaborative approach provides the opportunity for consistency in response and support mechanisms across all the environments of children who display harmful sexual behaviour. Enabling educators' access to support materials and practices not only assists the child with the behaviour, but also provides educators with informed strategies to manage and support the child whilst in their education setting. Such knowledge is also likely to inform educators of best practices for other children who may have been involved in or exposed to the behaviour.

Other treatment and interventions for children who display harmful sexual behaviour include cognitive behaviour therapy, including therapy specifically for sexual behaviour problems; trauma-focused, sexual abuse-specific therapy; gradual exposure; play therapy; expressive therapy; relapse prevention; group treatment; client-centred therapy; non-directive supportive

Responding to harmful sexual behaviour 85

therapy; and a multi-model intervention (Cox, Ey, Parkinson, & Bromfiel 2018). The delivery of these interventions may include sessions with the parent/caregiver and child, separate therapy sessions with parent/caregiver and child, and group therapy (Cox et al. 2018). Shlonsky et al. (2017) point out that although there are services available for children, accessibility of the services is sometimes problematic because of a lack of spaces in the program or the location of the services.

External support services for children who have harmful sexual behaviour

Briggs (2012) argues that schools and teachers are important figures in protecting children. She claims that well-informed educators can identify 'at risk' children, report suspicions, provide support and therapeutic activities to assist children's recovery or rehabilitation, support children and parents in seeking external support services, and provide preventative education. It is therefore important that educators have a sound understanding of healthy sexual development and sexual expression, as well as harmful sexual behaviour (Ey, McInnes, & Rigney 2017). It is also important for educators to familiarise themselves with support services available for children who display harmful sexual behaviour. There are currently limited specialist services for children with harmful sexual behaviours (Table 8.1);

Table 8.1 Specialist services for children with harmful sexual behaviours by jurisdiction

Jurisdiction	Intervention	Eligibility
New South Wales	New Street Adolescent Services	Children aged 10–17 not convicted of a sexual offence
New South Wales	Sexualised Behaviours (under 10s) Program (Sparks)	Children under 10 with problematic or harmful sexual behaviour
Victoria	Sexually Abusive Behaviour Treatment Services	Children aged up to 18 following voluntary or mandatory referral
Victoria	Male Adolescent Program for Positive Sexuality	Children and young people aged 10–12 convicted of a sexual offence
Queensland	Griffith Youth Forensic Service	Children convicted of a sexual offence
Queensland	Mater Family and Youth Counselling Service	Children convicted of a sexual offence

Source: Adapted from Royal Commission into Institutional Responses to Child Sexual Abuse 2017b, p. 180.

however, if access to specialised services proves difficult, educators should suggest mainstream services, such as:

- mental health services;
- community health services;
- specialised health services, such as SA Health: Sexual Health Services;
- general practitioners (GPs);
- private practitioners, such as psychologists.

(Royal Commission into Institutional Responses to Child Sexual Abuse 2017a)

It is essential that schools maintain up-to-date lists of local support services to enable educators or schools to provide information about relevant local services for children and parents if parents or children indicate a need to access these.

Initial responses

The Royal Commission into Institutional Responses to Child Sexual Abuse: Recommendations (Royal Commission into Institutional Responses to Child Sexual Abuse 2017c, p. 33) requires all state and territory governments to establish 'primary prevention strategies to educate family, community members, carers and professionals, including mandatory reporters, about preventing harmful sexual behaviours, and intervening when harmful sexual behaviours are developing or are already prevalent'. This initiative is particularly important for schools and educators as determined in Volume 10 of the Royal Commission into Institutional Responses to Child Sexual Abuse: Children with harmful sexual behaviours (Royal Commission into Institutional Responses to Child Sexual Abuse 2017b), which identified that staff in institutional contexts need the tools, resources, support, and training to respond appropriately to harmful sexual behaviour and facilitate early intervention.

It is important to recognise that children who display harmful sexual behaviours are, first and foremost, children (Meiksans, Bromfield, & Ey 2017). If an educator observes or receives a report of harmful sexual behaviour, it is essential that he or she remains calm and avoids panicked or shocked responses (Briggs 2012). Each state and territory education department will have different policies and procedures on how to respond, based on compliance with legislated requirements. The authors are most familiar with the South Australian education departmental policies and procedures and will therefore provide an overview of South Australia as a case study. Drawing on South Australia's *Responding to problem sexual behaviour in children and young people: Guidelines for staff in education and care settings (3rd edition)* (Department for Education 2019), the most important first response is to determine the severity of the behaviour. The behaviour needs to be reviewed relative to several factors. These include the age and developmental capability of the child or children (using the department resource of what constitutes typical sexual development and what behaviour is concerning or serious/problematic); the differences in age or developmental level of children involved; the context in which the behaviour has taken place (e.g. public versus private, or obstructing another child from leaving the location where the incident occurred); behaviour history of the child (ongoing behaviour, behaviour that is increasing in severity as opposed to a once-off incident); and the impact of the behaviour on others (e.g. penetrative behaviour, or potential social, psychological, or emotional impact) (Department for Education 2019).

In South Australia, there are procedures for immediate responses for the first staff member involved. These include attending to immediate safety needs, meaning providing first aid, securing the area to prevent or limit traffic, and alerting leadership or the emergency team. The staff member needs to respond calmly to children in their care, listen to accounts of what has occurred, and provide appropriate reassurance. From the information collected once the staff member has become aware of an incident, they need to establish the whereabouts of the other children involved and act to support the safety of all children. This may involve separating them, obtaining further supervision, or quarantining sexual material or other relevant evidence. Finally, they need to hand over the information to site leadership and begin documenting the incident (Department for Education 2019). For clear guidelines about documenting harmful sexual behaviour incidents, see Ey and Bromfield (2020). Site leadership is then responsible for contacting police if required, reporting the incident to child protection services, supervising the child or children involved, and contacting necessary others such as case workers or parents. The leadership is also responsible for reporting, documenting, and storing critical incident reports. It is their role to identify and inform other parents or guardians if required and, keeping within the information sharing policy, inform relevant others (e.g. boarding house director, child care or out-of-school hours care director), as well as recording the site's actions (Department for Education 2019).

Long-term responses

Whilst identifying and reporting harmful sexual behaviours are important first steps, there are ongoing demands for educators and other professionals to be able to restore and maintain the physical and emotional safety of children in care, learning, or service environments. Once an incident has occurred, it is important to continue monitoring the safety and wellbeing of children involved, to maintain communication with other agencies and professionals providing services, and to be responsive to the parents of the children involved (Department for Education 2019). In collaboration with relevant professionals, a behaviour support plan for the child exhibiting harmful sexual behaviour needs to be established, along with support and safety plans for other children involved. This is done to continue to enable a supportive response and to monitor the children's behaviour and wellbeing. It is important to consider who will need to be familiar with the behaviour and safety plan. If the behaviour does not improve, the site leadership team will need to initiate further planning with parents and=the required agencies (Department for Education 2019). If a child cannot remain at a site, leadership needs to seek support from the appropriate team in the department's head office. Site actions need to be recorded and reviewed in light of continuing the support and safety for children involved, as well as to inform future practice of the site's processes for responding to and preventing incidents (Department for Education 2019).

Behaviour support plan

A behaviour support plan is a formal, agreed set of actions that is developed between the site, the child who displayed harmful sexual behaviour, their parents, and involved agencies. The purpose of this plan is to outline the roles and responsibilities of all parties to support rehabilitation. A behaviour support plan may include a risk assessment of the child's behaviour; treatment, or supports provided by external agencies such as Child and Adolescent Mental Health Services; behaviour goals as well as methods of reinforcement; supervision provisions; boundaries relative to areas or other children; devised responses; an educative program; and agreed actions in response to not complying with the agreements (Department for Education 2019). The behaviour support plan brings key people together to work collaboratively to better support the child, whilst also providing the child with some agency.

Support and safety plan

A support and safety plan is a formal, agreed set of actions that is developed between the site, the child involved in or affected by harmful sexual behaviour, their parents, and involved agencies. The purpose of the plan is

Responding to harmful sexual behaviour 89

to outline the roles and responsibilities of all parties in helping the child to be and feel safe and supported (Department for Education 2019). A support and safety plan should include 'information about the requirements or restrictions that have been placed on the other child', agreed actions that the child will take if they feel unsafe or become aware that the other child is not complying with their behaviour plan, 'agreed actions that the parents will take if they feel their child is unsafe', any treatment or support that is being accessed, and communication methods between the agencies or professionals and the site. Importantly, it should also note the agreed indicators of stress (experienced by the child) that will be shared immediately between the child or young person, the site, parents, and any other professionals involved (Department for Education 2019, p. 24).

The behaviour support plan and the support safety plan reflect a multisystemic approach which is a highly recommended method in responding to children who have displayed or been affected by harmful sexual behaviour (Lloyd 2019).

Individual educators' support strategies

It is important to understand that educators are not trained psychologists or social workers; thus, their role is not to provide treatment to children. However, educators need to respond to children in a supportive manner. Research with young people aged 13–21 years ($n = 15$) found that those who were harmed by harmful sexual behaviour reported that they were more likely to disclose further harm and to trust teachers in cases in which schools responded effectively. It is well established that early intervention increases rehabilitative outcomes for the children involved (Meiksans et al. 2017; O'Brien 2010; Shlonsky et al. 2017). Educators who are responsive and supportive are more likely to be approached by children who may be at risk of harm. Additionally, educators who avoid stigmatising the child are more likely to provide a more effective response (O'Brien 2010). This is evident in Lloyd's (2019) research when one educator avoided labelling or stigmatising the child, but rather focused on the behaviour:

> It's educating rather than demonising, I think that's what we've got to remember, we've got to educate them, because they don't understand, rather than just punish them. If you've got a child that's been sexting and you exclude them for three days, they don't need to be excluded, they need to be taught why it's wrong, the law (school staff focus group).
>
> (Lloyd 2019, p. 7)

Children who engage in harmful sexual behaviour are likely to have come from backgrounds of trauma, adversity, disadvantage, or compromised social/educational engagement (O'Brien 2010). It is important that educators understand the indicators of stress, can respond appropriately to children experiencing trauma reactions, and are able to adapt their practices to meet children's needs. This requires shared understandings of trauma-informed practice. Donisch, Bray, and Gewirtz (2016) found that different professionals across education, mental health, child welfare, and juvenile justice had divergent understandings about trauma-informed practice. They argue that trauma-informed practice (Australian Childhood Foundation 2010) should be an important component of professional training and development to ensure that all practitioners share common language and understandings so that they are aware of the immediate and cumulative effects of traumatising exposures and their developmental implications for children.

Trauma-informed practice in education emphasises the construction of the school space, which provides predictable routines and safe relationships, and facilitates an environment that is flexible and conducive to the needs of all children, in particular those who are affected by trauma (Australian Childhood Foundation 2010). The Australian Childhood Foundation offers an online workshop for educators on trauma-informed practice, The SMART Program. This program aims to establish a supportive physical and emotional environment. The acronym PRACTICE is used to guide school counsellors, teachers, and others in how to respond and support children who have experienced abuse-related trauma (Australian Childhood Foundation 2006):

P – Predictable
R – Responsive
A – Attuned
C – Connecting
T – Translating
I – Involving
C – Calming
E – Engaging

Predictable: Traumatised children need a supportive and predictable environment that has a consistent routine so they can recognise patterns and more easily cope with transition (Australian Childhood Foundation 2006).

Responsive: Educators need to understand that traumatised children's behaviours reflect their coping strategies and should respond by using low-stress opportunities to reinforce rules, consequences, and behaviours. If an incident has occurred, it is important to talk through the incident and response strategies to shape positive behaviours. Educators need to acknowledge children's successes and improvements when the child does respond well to incidents. Finally, educators need to build strong relationships and stay connected with children (Australian Childhood Foundation 2006).

Attuned: Traumatised children may need support in tuning in to the way they are feeling. Educators need to support children in learning about, recognising, and understanding their feelings (Australian Childhood Foundation 2006).

Connecting: 'Traumatised children often feel disconnected from their feelings, their memories and their own sense of identity' (Australian Childhood Foundation 2006, p. 3). It is important that educators understand and acknowledge traumatised children's feelings and experiences, and role model and support children in self-regulating their feelings (Australian Childhood Foundation 2006).

Translating: As a result of children's previous experiences of abuse, they need support in developing their metacognitive and memory skills. Educators need to support children in building their memories and reviewing their experiences. They also need to support children in being able to recognise their qualities and envisage the future with qualities that they know about themselves in the present (Australian Childhood Foundation 2006).

Involving: Traumatised children have poor internal working models; this affects their ability to form, maintain, and understand relationships with others. Educators need to support children in developing co-operative and positive social skills. They also need to support and encourage traumatised children to develop strong peer relationships (Australian Childhood Foundation 2006).

Calming: Traumatised children are often in a state of elevated stress and need opportunities to learn how to relax and reach a calm state. Educators need to support children to identify ways to calm themselves and engage in soothing and physical activities, such as music, therapeutic play, and yoga (Australian Childhood Foundation 2006).

Engaging: Traumatised children may have difficulties relating to adults because of their previous experiences of being abused, not being protected or supported by an adult, and not learning how to trust. Educators need to build trusting and supportive relationships with children to enable them to feel a sense of belonging and provide children with a reliable, supportive adult in whom they can confide or turn to for support (Australian Childhood Foundation 2006).

Translating trauma-informed strategies in classrooms generally results in positive practices for all children and can therefore be implemented as a universal approach, rather than individually targeted (Whitington & McInnes 2017). Neurodevelopmental trauma researcher Bruce Perry (2020) identifies important attributes of an emotionally safe classroom.

Calm predictability in classrooms and in long day care sites includes keeping to routines or giving ample prior warning of changes to regular activities, timetables, or seating patterns. Calm voices and gestures avoid triggering children who have experienced loud voices and sudden movements as indicators of danger. All children respond well to calm adults and information about what they can expect, but such information is especially helpful for children who have experienced trauma to feel less anxious or fearful.

Behaviours arising from traumatic events can be confusing to educators and others because they often do not appear to relate to their immediate social environment (Streeck-Fischer & van der Kolk 2000). Being appropriately responsive to children's behaviour requires educator knowledge of how the body's physiological responses to trauma affect children's behaviour, as well as of each child's context and experiences.

Shutting down feelings is a protective response during traumatic experiences, particularly when these are repeated over time and the child has no prospect of escaping or stopping their experience. However, understanding their own behaviour and the behaviour of others requires children learning to identify and name their feelings (McInnes, Diamond, & Whitington 2015). Resources such as Kimochis (2020) are effective in developing children's emotional literacy and helping traumatised children become attuned to their feelings, enabling them to recognise how they affect their behaviour.

In developing and translating a positive self-identity for children who have come through experiences of pain and humiliation, Yuen (2007) provides narrative conversation strategies focusing on identifying the qualities children drew on to cope with and survive traumatising experiences. These conversations help children recognise their strengths and capacities.

Involving children in opportunities to develop a sense of self-efficacy may translate into children taking on helping roles in the classroom where they can succeed and feel valued. These could be tasks such as watering a pot plant or filling a pet feeder, taking a message, or checking a garden for vegetables. Being supported to make choices and feeling valued and successful are important contributors to a positive sense of self-identity and control (Perry 2020).

Talking with children when they are feeling calm about the ways they can help themselves relax is useful to making a plan with them for when they are feeling unsafe or upset (Perry 2020). Some children like to cocoon themselves in blankets or enclosed spaces such as cubby houses or tents. Others like tactile play with water, sand, or slinky fabrics. Some children might want to be outside in a garden or by themselves. Educators need to have an understanding of children's preferences and support children to build their calming resources (Briggs 2012). If children know they can use their calming strategies when they recognise stressed feelings, they are able to feel less anxious.

Taking time to build relationships with each child facilitates improved communication and trust. Being trustworthy includes being safe, calm, non-judgemental, available, and reliable – doing what you said you would do and being honest about your own behaviour. It also requires educators to always be respectful of children in their care.

Whole-school responses

Counselling

Children who have engaged in harmful sexual behaviour and those who have been affected need individual support. Schools need to ensure that children have access to counselling services within the school. Research by Lloyd (2019), who interviewed education staff, children, and staff working in multiagency partnerships, found that the students needed and appreciated having access to counselling services at school. One boy stated:

> The Student Support Centre's been really great for me. Yeah, the counsellors as well, the counsellors that I used to go to on a Wednesday, I'd always cry when I go there. I cried there twice (young people's focus group, boys).
>
> (Lloyd 2019, p. 9)

Physical environment

The physical environment of a school or education setting has been identified as a risk factor for harmful sexual behaviour (Lloyd 2019). Schools that made changes to the physical environment, such as prohibiting students from being in locations that had previously been an area of concern for sexual violence, and increasing CCTV or lighting around the school, appeared to make young people feel safer (Lloyd 2019). Other considerations for the physical environment are to lessen potential risk areas, such as thick shrubbery, and monitor areas that are renowned for harmful sexual behaviour, such as toilets (Briggs 2012).

Policies and procedures

As outlined earlier, the Royal Commission into Institutional Responses to Child Sexual Abuse has recommended that institutions that work with children, including schools, have strong policies and procedures in place to prevent and respond to child sexual abuse and harmful sexual behaviour (Royal Commission into Institutional Responses to Child Sexual Abuse 2017c). Such policies should be made publicly available, and it is essential that all educators are familiar with these. School staff felt confident in responding to harmful sexual behaviour when their school had strong policies and procedures, as well as continuous and relevant staff development programs (Lloyd 2019).

Peer support

Children may not always feel comfortable speaking with educators or seeking help from adults, especially traumatised children (Australian Childhood Foundation 2006). Peers, therefore, may play a significant role in supporting one another if involved in harmful sexual behaviour. Lloyd (2019, p. 9) found that 'in addition to formal support structures within the school itself, young people noted the importance of friendships with peers to offering support, advice and informal interventions'. Peers can provide emotional support, intervene in harmful incidents, and support one another's ongoing welfare (Lloyd 2019).

Education

Child protection educational programs delivered within schools aim to promote responsible and respectful relationships among children and teach children about respectful behaviours. Although education is designed to be a preventative strategy to harmful sexual behaviour, several young people who had exhibited harmful sexual behaviour stated that they received sex education too late, after they had sexually offended (McKibbin, Humphreys, & Hamilton 2017). One male stated:

> I think if I had sex education before everything had occurred, like obviously before I hit full on puberty, I think everything would have changed. I think, I'm not even sure if what had happened would have happened, because I would have known it was wrong, more so than what I did at the time. I would have known why it was wrong and why not to do it.
>
> (McKibbin et al. 2017, p. 214)

Another young male stated:

> Before [puberty] occurs or definitely, what's been brought up is ... get the school and the parents into sex education and do it before [puberty] occurs. So at 10 and 11 [years old] even though puberty might be reached later on.
>
> (McKibbin et al. 2017, p. 215)

This research demonstrates that sex education needs to be introduced earlier. However, given that these children did not receive such education before their offences, it is important that they are taught about respectful relationships and respectful behaviours to prevent further incidents of harmful sexual behaviour.

Conclusion

Educators play a key role in supporting the rehabilitation and safety of children who engage in harmful sexual behaviour and those who have been affected. The way educators respond to harmful sexual behaviour could significantly affect the subsequent health and development of the children involved. Initial responses to incidents of harmful sexual behaviour need to be sensitive, whilst ensuring the safety of each child involved. Families and professionals in education and care, health services, family support services, therapeutic programs, police, and child protection need to be able to come together to establish safety and support behaviour changes in children displaying harmful sexual behaviour and aid the rehabilitation of children affected by harmful sexual behaviour (Evertsz & Miller 2012). Each phase of the report, support plans, and monitoring need to be thoroughly documented and reviewed to maintain children's safety and inform future practice. Educators need to respond to the behaviour rather than stigmatising the child and provide a safe and supportive environment for all children. Trauma-informed practice as a universal standard is a key approach to responding effectively to children who have been involved in harmful sexual behaviour, whilst implementing a best practice environment for all children.

References

Australian Bureau of Statistics 2018, *Schools, Australia*, Australian Bureau of Statistics, Canberra <www.abs.gov.au/ausstats/abs@.nsf/Latestproducts/4221.0Main%20Features22017?opendocument&tabname=Summary&prodno=4221.0&issue=2017&num=&view=>.

Australian Childhood Foundation 2006, *Responding to children who have experienced abuse related trauma: Ideas for school based treatment*, Richmond, Victoria, <https://professionals.childhood.org.au/app/uploads/2018/08/SMART-Discussion-Paper-1-1.pdf>.

Australian Childhood Foundation 2010, *Making space for learning: Trauma informed practice in schools*, Richmond, Victoria, <www.childhood.org.au/forprofessionals/resources>.

Australian Institute of Family Studies 2017a, *Mandatory reporting of child abuse and neglect* Australian Institute of Family Studies, Southbank, Victoria, viewed 6 September, <https://aifs.gov.au/cfca/publications/mandatory-reporting-child-abuse-and-neglect>.

Australian Institute of Family Studies 2017b, *Child protection Australia 2016–2017*, Canberra, <www.aihw.gov.au/getmedia/66c7c364-592a-458c-9ab0-f90022e25368/aihw-cws-63.pdf.aspx?inline=true>.

Briggs, F 2012, *Child protection: The essential guide for teachers and other professionals whose work involves children*, Jo-Jo Publishing, Docklands, Victoria.

Cox, S, Ey, L, Parkinson, S & Bromfield, L 2018, *Service models for children under 10 with problematic sexual behaviours: An Evidence Check rapid review brokered by the Sax Institute for the NSW Ministry of Health*, Sydney, <www.health.nsw.gov.au/parvan/sexualassault/Documents/service-models-under10.PDF>.

Department for Education 2019, *Responding to problem sexual behaviour in children and young people: Guidelines for staff in education and care settings (3rd edition)*, Government of South Australia: Department for Education, South Australia.

Donisch, K, Bray, C & Gewirtz, A 2016, 'Child welfare, juvenile justice, mental health, and education providers' conceptualizations of trauma-informed practice', *Child Maltreatment*, vol. 21, no. 2, pp. 125–134.

Evertsz, J & Miller, R 2012, *Children with problem sexual behaviours and their families: Best interests case practice model: Specialist practice resource*, Melbourne, Department of Human Services.

Ey, L, McInnes, E & Rigney, L 2017, 'Educators' understanding of young children's typical and problematic sexual behaviour and their training in this area', *Sex Education*, vol. 17, no. 6, pp. 682–696.

Kimochis 2020, viewed 8 January 2020, <www.kimochis.com/> .

Lloyd, J 2019, 'Response and interventions into harmful sexual behaviour in schools', *Child Abuse & Neglect*, vol. 94.

McInnes, E, Diamond, A & Whitington, V 2015, 'Embedding wellbeing and creating community in classrooms', in Karl Brettig (ed), *Building stronger communities with children and families*, Cambridge Scholars Publishing, Newcastle on Tyne.

McKibbin, G, Humphreys, C & Hamilton, B 2017, '"Talking about child sexual abuse would have helped me": Young people who sexually abuse reflect on preventing harmful sexual behaviour', *Child Abuse & Neglect*, vol. 70, pp. 210–221.

Meiksans, J, Bromfield, L & Ey, L 2017, *A continuum of responses for harmful sexual behaviours*, Commissioner for Children and Young People, Western

Australia, Perth, <www.ccyp.wa.gov.au/media/2973/a-continuum-of-responses-for-harmful-sexual-behaviours-australian-centre-for-child-protection-april-2018.pdf>.

Ministerial Council on Education: Early Childhood Development and Youth Affairs 2011, *National safe schools framework*, Education Services Australia, Carlton South, Victoria.

O'Brien, W 2010, *Australia's response to sexualised or sexually abuse behaviours in children and young people*, Australian Crime Commission, Canberra, ACT, <http://dro.deakin.edu.au/eserv/DU:30065114/obrien-australias-2010.pdf>.

Perry, BD 2020, 'Emotional development: Creating an emotionally safe classroom', *Scholastic.com*, <www.scholastic.com/teachers/articles/teaching-content/emotional-development-creating-emotionally-safe-classroom/>.

Royal Commission into Institutional Responses to Child Sexual Abuse 2016, *Institutional responses to child sexual abuse in out-of-home care: Consultation paper*, Sydney, <www.childabuseroyalcommission.gov.au/consultation-papers>.

Royal Commission into Institutional Responses to Child Sexual Abuse 2017a, *Final report: Children with harmful sexual behaviours*, Commonwealth of Australia, Canberra, <www.childabuseroyalcommission.gov.au/sites/default/files/final_report_-_volume_10_children_with_harmful_sexual_behaviours.pdf>.

Royal Commission into Institutional Responses to Child Sexual Abuse 2017b, *Final Report: Advocacy, support and therapeutic treatment services*, Canberra, <www.childabuseroyalcommission.gov.au/sites/default/files/final_report_-_volume_9_advocacy_support_and_therapeutic_treatment_services.pdf>.

Royal Commission into Institutional Responses to Child Sexual Abuse 2017c, *Final report: Recommendations*, Commonwealth of Australia, Canberra, <www.childabuseroyalcommission.gov.au/recommendations>.

Shlonsky, A, Albers, B, Tolliday, D, Wilson, S, Norvell, J & Kissinger, L 2017, *Rapid evidence assessment: Current best evidence in the therapeutic treatment of children with problem or harmful sexual behaviours, and children who have sexually offended*, Royal Commission into Institutional Responses to Child Sexual Abuse, Sydney, <www.childabuseroyalcommission.gov.au/policy-and-research/our-research/publishedresearch/therapeutic-treatment-of-children-with-problem-or>.

Skovdal, M & Campbell, C 2015, 'Beyond education: What role can schools play in the support and protection of children in extreme settings?', *International Journal of Educational Development*, vol. 41, pp. 175–183.

Streeck-Fischer, A & van der Kolk, B 2000, 'Down will come baby, cradle and all: Diagnostic and therapeutic implications of chronic trauma on child development', *Australian and New Zealand Journal of Psychiatry*, vol. 34, no. 6, pp. 903–918.

Yuen, A 2007, 'Discovering children's responses to trauma: A response based narrative practice', *The International Journal of Narrative Therapy and Community Work*, vol. 4, pp. 3–18.

Whitington, V & McInnes, E 2017, 'Developing a "classroom as community" approach to supporting young children's well-being', *Australasian Journal of Early Childhood*, vol. 42, no. 4, pp. 22–29, <https://doi.org/10.23965/AJEC.42.4.03>.

9 Identifying challenges and prevention strategies

Introduction

The identification, response, management, and prevention of harmful sexual behaviours is an ongoing project. It necessarily involves many more people and agencies than the individual child and a single treating professional, including the child's parents and other family members, their educators or carers, their peers and directly affected children, the families of those children, child protection staff, education and/or health department staff, treating therapists, and potentially police and legal staff. These varied individuals and groups come together in different ways over time relating to each incident (Donisch, Bray, & Gewirtz 2016). Educators, and other professionals working with children, are hindered in their ability to recognise and respond to children involved in harmful sexual behaviour, owing to several key challenges. For example, many professionals have limited understanding of children's sexual development and the behaviours that constitute age-appropriate and harmful sexual behaviour across different developmental stages (Meiksans, Bromfield, & Ey 2017). Additionally, many professionals have limited awareness of the potential complexities affecting children who display harmful sexual behaviour. The responses of child protection and criminal justice may act as a deterrent for seeking help for children, because of fear of children being removed from their families and criminal culpability for children aged 10–17 years (Meiksans et al. 2017). Each child's experience of their behaviour and its aftermath is critical to shaping the child's trajectory – either into opportunities for safety and recovery along with changes in their environment and behaviour, or continuing harmful sexual behaviours which could persist into later childhood and affect many more children (Burton 2000). This chapter examines the contexts and challenges of preventing harmful sexual behaviours and supporting positive outcomes for the children affected by harmful sexual behaviours.

Revisiting children's vulnerabilities through an ecological systems approach

A key question which has challenged the understanding of harmful sexual behaviours is the search for causes, in order to better understand how to constrain and prevent harmful sexual behaviours, and to support children to change their behaviour. Harmful sexual behaviours can be understood on a continuum of severity of impact on the child engaging in these behaviours and others who are affected by them (Australian Institute of Family Studies 2017). The level of impact relates not only to the behaviour, but also to the context and experiences of each child. Lynch and Cicchetti (1998) argue that an ecological model can assist in identifying risk and protective factors in a child's environment, as well as the child's level of *ontogenic* development (1998, p. 236) in adaptation to their circumstances. It is therefore important to gain insight into the child as well as their context, including their household; parenting dynamics; family networks, cultural norms, and practices; community connections to schools; child care, religious, and recreation groups; as well as the family's broader socio-economic interaction with social institutions such as the labour market, welfare system, or criminal justice system. Together these shape children's daily interactions which combine to form their cognitive and behavioural relationship with their environment. Attention to the environment that has shaped children's behaviours is vital in supporting children to recover from impacts of harmful sexual behaviours and to help the child acting out harmful sexual behaviours (Australian Childhood Foundation 2010).

The diagram of Bronfenbrenner's (1979) model in Figure 9.1 provides a model for mapping the child's contexts across these spheres of influence.

Bronfenbrenner's Bio-Ecological Systems Theory places a heavy emphasis on the bidirectional interactions between the person and the environment which shape learning and development (Griffore & Phenice 2016). Proximal processes are the development processes of systematic interaction between person and environment and include Process-Person-Context-Time.

Children's personal characteristics and resources have the potential to alter, create, or evoke a response from the external environment, thereby influencing the subsequent course of their psychological growth (Bronfenbrenner 2005). There are three 'person' characteristics: disposition (e.g. initiative, responsiveness versus impulsivity, distraction), resource (e.g. ability, knowledge, skill, versus disability, severe and persistent illness, or poor brain function), and demand (e.g. difficult or calm temperament, attractive versus unattractive appearance, hyperactivity and passivity, age, gender, and skin colour) (Bronfenbrenner 2005; Rosa & Tudge 2013). Children's dispositions, resources, and temperaments thus affect the way children

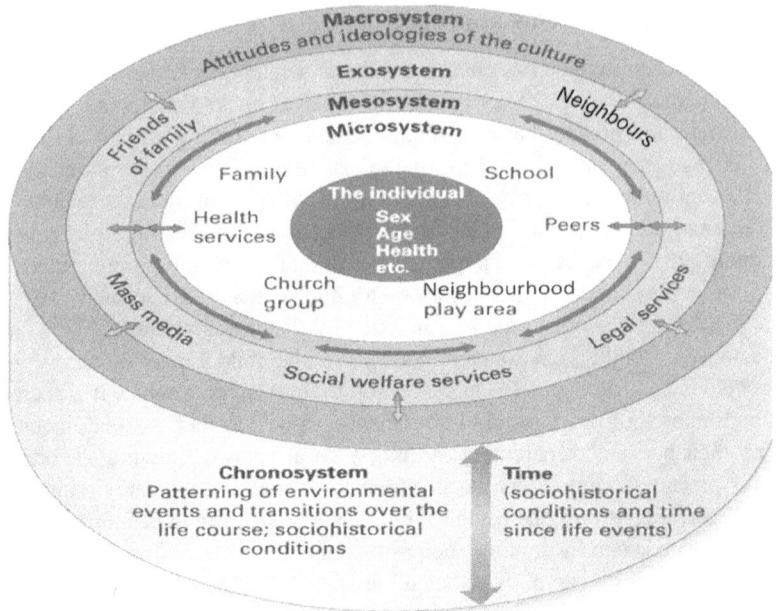

Figure 9.1 Bronfenbrenner's Bio-Ecological Systems Theory (Peterson 2010)

encounter their world and how others respond to them. Rothbart (2007 p. 207) notes that

> Temperament and experience together 'grow' a personality, which will include the child's developing cognitions about self, others, and the physical and social world, as well as his or her values, attitudes, and coping strategies.

According to Rosa and Tudge (2013), two or more forces produce an effect that is greater than the sum of the individual effects. In relation to person-context, the person and context characteristics are considered jointly. Favourable and non-favourable environments influence the development of individuals with particular personal characteristics (Bronfenbrenner 2005). The process-person-context relates to developmental outcomes as a product of interactions of the person with their context, thereby emphasising the effectiveness of the process towards the developmental outcome. Finally, the process-person-context-time includes timing of the event and the era (Bronfenbrenner 2005; Rosa & Tudge 2013). These proximal processes therefore shape the systems in which children grow.

Challenges and prevention strategies 101

This means that the ways children understand and respond to their experiences and interactions can affect their vulnerability to engaging in harmful sexual behaviours. Elkovitch et al. (2009, p. 593) identify that temperament is recognised as a factor in the development of psychopathology in children but needs further research for the dynamic relationship to be better understood.

The individual characteristics of children, including their gender, age, health status, and temperament, together affect their own capacities to learn, respond, and adapt (their *ontogenic* development), and organise how the people in their lives interact with them in a variety of contexts (Bowes & Hayes 2004). Gender is a defining characteristic of children in most cultures. Children are classified at birth as male or female, and this is culturally translated into an expected set of characteristic features and behaviours which will shape their interactions with significant others. Significantly, such culturally assigned characteristics and expectations identify sex roles and sexual behaviour. Parents' beliefs about ideal masculinity and femininity translate into colour-coded clothing, gendered toys (Auster & Mansbach 2012), activities, and practices of relationship. For example, notions such as 'boys don't cry', 'be tough', and 'don't be a sook' can mean that male children receive less emotional comfort when distressed (Fivush 1991). Boys are also more likely than girls to come to the attention of the child protection system in Australia for physical abuse (AIHW 2019). Boys may also be treated as 'being the boss' or 'the little man of the house', with support for assertive behaviours. In the case of girls, cultural beliefs that they are less important than males and should be obedient to them, or they should 'be pretty' and 'nice' and expected to learn how to present themselves as sexually desirable to males contribute to higher rates of sexual abuse of girls recorded consistently in Australia's child protection system (AIHW 2019). Harmful sexual behaviour affects both boys and girls; however, the proportion of boys in the population of children identified as engaging in harmful sexual behaviours increases as children get older (Briggs 2012). Age is also significant to the vulnerability of children to developing harmful sexual behaviours. Elkovitch et al. (2009, p. 591) note that for children with a history of child sexual abuse, harmful sexual behaviours were most prevalent in the youngest age group of under 5 years. The onset of child sexual abuse before the age of 3 was the strongest predictor of harmful sexual behaviours for both boys and girls. Children with intellectual disabilities have been identified as being at greater risk of harmful sexual behaviours because of their cognitive and communicative vulnerabilities and higher levels of dependency on others (Briggs 2012; Evertsz & Kirsner 2003). Children with intellectual disabilities are less able to manage personal boundaries and impulse control and are themselves at greater risk of sexual abuse.

The child's *microsystem* is the environment that children inhabit on a daily or regular basis and includes their homes, education settings, neighbourhoods, and extra-curricular activities (Bronfenbrenner 1979). In the family environment, the treatment of the child, dynamics among family members, the quality of parenting, socio-economic circumstances, and sexual behaviours in the home influence children's developing awareness of their identity and the norms and expectations of interpersonal interactions. Growing up in a violent, abusive, or neglectful environment impedes children's development of self-esteem and self-regulation and is correlated with higher levels of externalising behaviours of aggression and impulsivity, which can include harmful sexual behaviours (Smith, Lindsey, Bohora, & Silovsky 2019). Children engaging in harmful sexual behaviours share multiple exposures to complex traumas at an early age, often directly linked to their experiences of parenting and care in their home environment. Children's problematic behaviours can escalate if educators are not trained to identify and respond appropriately to these complexities. Their relationships with families are essential to be able to work collaboratively to support children's holistic development. Such relationships are part of the child's *mesosystem*. The mesosystem mediates the interactions between the child's microsystem (e.g. teachers, children, and their families) and the *exosystem*, in which the child is not an active participant but is affected by the factors present in that system, such as child protection departments (Bronfenbrenner 1979). Harmful sexual behaviours are more often reported to authorities by professionals in settings outside the home as children mingle with peers and attend care, education, and community activities (AIHW 2019). Behaviours of concern may have been unnoticed, normalised, or ignored in the home environment, but become visible and reportable as children move into different social contexts. Violence or abuse in the community, ranging from bullying from peers to witnessing violent crime or being targeted by predatory adults, is also recognised as contributing to a further layer of risk factors for children, particularly those who have already experienced maltreatment at home (Lynch & Cicchetti 1998; Streeck-Fischer & van der Kolk 2000). Lynch and Cicchetti (1998, p. 244) identified that child maltreatment rates were higher in communities with higher rates of violence, compared with children living in communities with lower rates of violence. The distribution of family services and amenities, policing, and safe design affects the level of support available to families. The exosystem can thus exacerbate and deepen risks for children who have experienced maltreatment or neglect, or, conversely, provide protective opportunities for children through safe neighbourhoods, positive learning experiences, and social environments. Communities with accessible family support services, amenities for children to safely play outdoors, local networks with extended family and friends, health and education services, safe public transport routes, and sport, recreation, and cultural amenities enable parents and children to develop social connections. These are protective for children's wellbeing and thus a primary strategy for preventing and reducing child maltreatment (McInnes & Diamond 2011).

The broader cultural context of the *macrosystem* is shaped by, and shapes, the attitudes and beliefs which inform social understandings, parenting behaviours, and responses to children through the child protection system. For example, culturally dominant beliefs about smacking of children, children's ability to provide reliable witness evidence in legal proceedings, and views on whether parents' abuse of children should result in loss of care are examples of attitudes, beliefs, and practices of social workers and law professionals that shape the types of responses of child protection, criminal, and family law to children experiencing maltreatment. Statutory decisions that leave young children exposed to continuing physical and/or sexual abuse increase the risks to the child's development and their later risks of harmful sexual behaviours, sexually abusive behaviours, and potential criminalisation.

Social and economic status also influences families' capacities to reliably meet children's basic needs and the degree of state intervention in their lives. In Australia, Indigenous children are much more likely to experience contact with the child protection and juvenile justice systems than the broader population (AIHW 2019). Intergenerational dispossession and loss of land, language, culture, children, wages, and freedom of movement and association have generated 'trauma trails' (Atkinson 2002) for Aboriginal and Torres Strait Islander peoples of Australia, manifesting in significant gaps between Indigenous and non-Indigenous Australians in life expectancy, child mortality, education, and employment (FHCSIA 2010). The impacts of intergenerational cumulative trauma were reflected in a recent report exploring key issues within the Aṉangu Pitjantjatjara Yankunytjatjara Lands of Aboriginal peoples, which found that 80% of children surveyed displayed harmful sexual behaviour (Parliament of South Australia 2019).

There are conflicting legal responses to children who experience violence and abuse. Children whose parents have separated can be ordered by the Australian family law system to spend time with parents convicted of family violence and/or child sex abuse (McInnes 2014), whereas under state and territory child protection laws, children are likely to be removed from homes where they are exposed to family violence and/or sexual abuse (AIHW 2019). Convicted child sex offenders are prevented from working or volunteering with children, but family law does allow for them to have care of their biological children.

Similarly, Australian child protection laws recognise the harms of children's exposure to family violence, yet mothers and children living with violent partners and fathers face limited opportunities for income support, housing, or safety if they separate (McInnes 2015). Attitudes to violence against women shape the level of acceptance in the community for legal protections from abuse in relationships. The 2017 National Community Attitudes towards Violence Against Women Survey (or NCAS) (Webster et al. 2019) identified that one in three Australians think it is 'natural' for a man to want to appear to be in charge of his female partner in front of his friends. Such views reveal the levels of cultural support for gender dynamics which involve the use of coercive force. Domestic and family violence is effectively decriminalised in Australia through the use of civil restraining orders as a first response, in preference to criminal prosecution for assault, which would apply in cases where there was no personal relationship. Preventing and reducing family violence requires proactive policing and legal responses that prioritise safety of victims and accountability for offenders (McInnes 2015).

The challenges of reducing cultural support for and practices of family violence and child maltreatment underpin the difficulties of preventing harmful sexual behaviours linked with histories of complex trauma involving multiple forms of maltreatment (Mesman, Harper, Edge, Brandt, & Pemberton 2019; Smith et al. 2019). These challenges are amplified in the current digital age of instant access to internet and media content which enables rapid circulation of violent and/or sexual content involving adults and children.

Challenges from media and technologies

Media play a key role in shaping public attitudes and understanding (McHale, Dotterer, & Kim 2009) and can thus be recognised as a key institution of both the macrosystem and the *chronosystem*. The chronosystem can be understood as the temporal (time) dimension of the model. It reflects the dynamic environmental transitions within the culture that occur over time (Bronfenbrenner 2005). In this context, the rise in technology over time and the increased ease of access to sexualised media are contributing factors to the rise of child exploitation, and consequently, harmful sexual behaviours.

McHale et al. (2009) argue that young people engage with media as part of their daily activities in learning and practicing skills, identity development, and building social connections. Over the past two decades, access

Challenges and prevention strategies 105

to the internet in homes with children under age 15 has risen to 97% of Australian households in 2016–17, with 99% of these connected households using a mobile or smart phone to access the internet (ABS 2018). Computers and smartphones were the most commonly used devices, ahead of tablets, internet-connected televisions, music and video players, and gaming consoles. For households with children aged under 15 years, the mean number of devices used was 7.8, compared with 5.4 devices per connected household without children aged under 15 (ABS 2018). These data show the scale of connectivity in households with preschool- and school-aged children, as well as the complexities for parents attempting to keep track of their child's exposure to online content.

Online entertainment, streaming and on-demand content, social media, and online gaming have transformed adults' and children's experiences of media consumption, enabling more personalised selection of viewing, listening, and gaming activities than free-to-air scheduled programming. The technological revolution has also opened new dangers for children. Children living in households with consumers of online adult pornography can be incidentally or intentionally exposed to such content. In 2016–17, 14% of connected households with children aged 5–14 stated a child had been exposed to inappropriate material, and 5% of these households stated a child aged 5–14 had been subject to cyberbullying (ABS 2018). Flood (2007) identified that amongst Australian 16- and 17-year-olds, 75% had been exposed accidentally to pornographic websites, whilst 38% of boys and 2% of girls had deliberately accessed them. In the same age group, 75% of boys and 10% of girls had watched an X-rated movie. The internet has created new opportunities for shaping attitudes by enabling the sharing of information and content among like-minded groups, ranging from interests in everyday activities such as craft or gardening to dangerous and illegal activities, including the production and circulation of child exploitation material. Current regulations prohibit certain types of sexually explicit content from being accessed online, such as child exploitation material or bestiality. Other types of sexually explicit content, including simulated sexual activity, are restricted to adults only (Internet Industry Association 2008). Although these regulations attempt to prevent minors from accessing explicit content online, it is not possible to monitor all of the sexually explicit content uploaded online. Therefore, the Australian regulatory scheme cannot be adequately enforced. Media regulation provides ratings and age limits on content consumption; however, media consumption in the private domain is controlled, if at all, by parents. Additionally, a review of the Australian and United States curricula that explored media literacy education for primary school–aged children 'found that while curriculum in both countries guide teachers in their education of primary school aged children to become critical viewers, listeners and creators of media, education about media influences on personal development is very limited' (Ey 2017, p. 116). Education on sensitive or controversial topics, such as sexualised media and pornography, was absent in primary school curriculum (Ey 2017). Given that research has demonstrated that children as young as 5 years old are imitating sexualised behaviour they are seeing in music videos (Ey & Cupit 2013), it is important that critical media literacy is embedded in curricula from an early age as a strategy to prevent problematic sexualised behaviour.

Easy, immediate, private access to global internet networks has enabled the proliferation of both online adult pornography and production and circulation of child exploitation content. A study of 152 Australians convicted of possessing child exploitation material identified that all offenders were men, with most aged between 46 and 55, and a median collection size of 1,000 files, with one in four having more than 10,000 files and 5% having more than 100,000 files involving sexual offending against children (Krone & Smith 2017, p. 7). The researchers identified that 86.2% of the offenders possessing child exploitation material did not have convictions for grooming or contact offences. Of those with a criminal history of multiple child sex exploitation offences, membership of a child exploitation material network was significantly linked to contact offending, particularly for those involved in producing and providing images to the network (Krone & Smith 2017, p. 10). The children who are involved in production of online child exploitation material experience multiple layers of victimisation in the experiences involved in capturing the images, the online circulation of their images, and the impacts on their behaviour and development, including the increased risk for displaying harmful sexual behaviours. Australia's eSafety Commissioner (www.esafety.gov.au) provides information and support to children, parents, and other social groups regarding prevention and reporting online problem behaviours, including grooming, sexting and image-based abuse, online bullying, stalking, and illegal content.

Training for educators and other professionals

Those who provide training resources for educators and other professionals in responding to and preventing harmful sexual behaviours face specific challenges of their own. These can include the complexities of children's individual circumstances, the diversity of families and their communities, different and changing legislative provisions, access to suitable therapeutic services, and finding ways to deliver what is needed by educators and other professionals, children, and families.

Preventing harmful sexual behaviours from occurring at all is extremely difficult in a social environment in which family violence and child maltreatment are prevalent concerns, and in which child exploitation material continues to proliferate on the internet. Educators and other professionals working with children need to be able to identify age-typical sexual behaviours consistent with normal development, as well as those which cause concern and those which cause harm (Department for Education 2019b; Ey, McInnes, & Rigney 2017).

Whilst police and educators are the professional groups most likely to report harmful sexual behaviours, apart from family members, other groups include health and social work professionals, and child protection and community services staff (Briggs 2012). The range of professional practitioners working with children and families can result in confusion and divergent views in understanding what has happened in the child's life, as well as in appropriate ways to respond to harmful sexual behaviours (Evertsz & Miller 2012). It is therefore important that the lead agency in response, usually statutory child protection services, works in partnership with the staff at affected sites.

Child and family education

The family environment is key to engaging with children, since the adults in a child's household shape the experiences and relationship dynamics of the child's learning environment. Children and their family members need to be able to identify ways to support children's safety within the physical and emotional environment. Trust relationships are central to effective communication by educators, carers, social workers, and therapists with children and their family members. Establishing trust relationships requires time, persistence, and authentic communication that recognises the strengths of families and children and avoids blame and judgement (Evertsz & Miller 2012, p. 25).

Children need to learn the names of their body parts and their rights over their bodies, and they need a trusted network of people to whom they can turn for help (Briggs 2012). In Australia, every state and territory has a child protection education curriculum. In South Australia the *Keeping safe: Child protection curriculum* (Department for Education 2019a) is taught in all schools to children from ages 3–18 and focuses on age-appropriate information about safe relationships and problem-solving ways to stay safe. Learning the names of body parts enables young children to describe their bodies and experiences. Learning about safe and unsafe touch, private body parts, and their rights over their bodies empowers children to refuse unwanted touching. Having a trusted network of safe, helpful adults supports children to tell others what has happened (Briggs with McVeity 2000). Books such as *Everybody's got a bottom* (Rowley & Edwards 2007) provide these key messages in a format suitable for young children.

For older primary school–age children, the *Keeping safe: Child protection curriculum* (Department for Education 2019a) builds on children's understanding of their right to be safe. Some of the content most relevant for preventing harmful sexual behaviour includes addressing safe and unsafe feelings; physical, emotional, and external warning signs; grooming; safe and unsafe touching; psychological pressure and manipulation; healthy and unhealthy relationships; sharing of inappropriate material; sexting; and protective strategies (Department for Education 2019a). However, whilst this education could work well as a preventative strategy for harmful sexual behaviour and child sexual abuse, there is no research that has explored how often the child protection curriculum is taught in schools, whether all students receive this education each year, whether every topic is covered each year to build on previous content, or whether the curriculum is effective in developing children's understanding and protective practices.

By involving parents and carers in children's learning about safety, they are enabled to share children's learning and to support that learning by using the same language and strategies. It is important to ensure that children from homes speaking languages other than English have access to key child safety messaging in their first language, with parents informed about the content of child protection information in that language. By educating parents about children's vulnerabilities to abuse, they can be better aware of the risks to their children and to indicators of abuse (Briggs with McVeity 2000, p. 18). Parents can also be exposed to information about children's developmental stages and abilities, which can in turn assist with appropriate expectations for toileting and sleep behaviours and to adopt parenting behaviours that reduce risks of abuse. Briggs with McVeity (2000, p. 20) argue that parents often underestimate risks to their children and may also be concerned that their children will be prematurely exposed to information about sex, or become fearful or disobedient if the children learn they have rights. Briggs and McVeity recommend that parent information sessions about child safety learning be followed up with workshops to give opportunities for parents to discuss strategies to put into practice, such as problem-solving safety concerns with their children (Briggs with McVeity 2000, p. 25). Child safety sessions also support parents to respond effectively to their child if they have concerns about their child's sexual behaviour, and how to make a report if their child discloses abuse, or if there are other indicators of concern.

Research into non-offending parents' responses to children's disclosures of sexual abuse has been found to vary according to whether or not the

Challenges and prevention strategies 109

alleged offender is external to the family. Elliott and Carnes' (2001) review of the research found that non-offending parents experienced shock and distress when children disclosed sexual abuse, and that, whilst most mothers believed their children and took protective action, this was more likely when they were not in a current sexual relationship with the alleged offender. Elliott and Carnes cite research by Pintello and Zuravin (2001, p. 316) which found that just over 41% of mothers believed and acted protectively, around 30% of mothers neither believed nor acted protectively, and the remainder was ambivalent, either not believing but still taking action, or believing but taking no action. Just over half the group classified as ambivalent still took protective action despite not believing their child.

If their children have been impacted by harmful sexual behaviour, parents can support them in their recovery by learning about how best to respond supportively in order to establish safety and offer comfort and reassurance.

Decreasing the physical context risk: physical setting and design

Although not all instances of harmful sexual behaviour involve physical contact among children, the design of the physical environment is a vital component of managing children's personal safety at care and education sites (Cradock, O'Donnell, Benjamin, Walker, & Slining 2010). Fencing, lighting, and hazard reduction are recognised elements of safety design, but it is equally important to ensure that staff are able to effectively supervise children at all times.

Key consideration should be given to ensuring that staff are able to maintain a line of sight across all areas of children's activity. Secrecy, along with coercion and aggression, is recognised as a common element of harmful sexual behaviours (Department for Education 2019b, p. 7; O'Brien 2008, p. 8). Keeping children in sight can deter harmful sexual behaviour, or, if it occurs, staff witnesses can intervene, respond to stop the behaviour, and provide details of what has occurred in making a report. Risk assessments of site layout and supervision arrangements should be an ongoing part of the management of care in education settings. Opportunities for interaction among children of different age groups and areas with limited visual access need to be identified and managed to support children's safety (Department for Education 2019b). When planning for events at the site, such as family barbecues, sleep-overs, or excursions, risks to safety must be considered and managed to ensure children and site visitors are appropriately supervised.

Planning for safety enables staff to place children in specific sections of the site to ensure that all children affected by harmful sexual behaviours are supported, and that the child displaying harmful sexual behaviour is managed to reduce the risk of future harmful sexual behaviour. Some sites will exclude children who have displayed harmful sexual behaviour. These assessments will be made by site leaders on a case-by-case basis depending on the context, severity, and impact of the behaviour, as well as on the amenities and affordances of the site (Department for Education 2019b). If a child attends an alternative site following a harmful sexual behaviour incident, the site leader needs to be informed of the relevant information in the history of the case. Staff responsible for supervising students need to be aware of safety plans to manage the child's behaviour. Site reviews following a critical incident aim to identify ways to contain risks of harmful sexual behaviour relating to all children at the site and to children displaying such behaviour. Safety planning needs to specify the actions to be taken and those responsible for the actions and include regular reviews of the efficacy of the plan (Department for Education 2019b).

Conclusion

There are many challenges in preventing and responding to harmful sexual behaviour. There is an ongoing need to educate professionals and parents in being able to identify harmful sexual behaviour and to develop understanding of the impacts of complex trauma on children's development and behaviour (Australian Childhood Foundation 2010). Families with parenting behaviours which result in young children's exposures to coercion and violence, sexual experience, neglect, and other forms of maltreatment can feel shamed or stigmatised. They may also be defensive or resistant to interventions to manage children's harmful sexual behaviours, requiring professionals with skills to engage with families in a non-judgemental way that nevertheless directly communicates the need to manage the child's behaviour and work together for change. Preventing and reducing family violence, and all forms of child maltreatment, is an ongoing, fundamental challenge, but it is vital to reduce and prevent harmful sexual behaviour.

Educating and empowering children to understand their rights over their body and their emotional responses can support behaviour changes and their capacities to form safe, positive social relationships with their peers. Involving parents in children's learning of safety strategies improves their knowledge of the risks to children and the actions they can take to support their children's safety. Parents need to know how to identify behaviours of concern and what to do if these occur, including making a report to child protection services.

Legal reforms are needed to improve accountability for abuse perpetrators and to protect children from abusive parents, along with increased government commitment to protecting children from exposures to images of violence, abuse, and sexually explicit content.

It is also vital for regulators and organisation leaders to ensure that education and care sites, and other services with responsibilities for care of children, such as hospitals or residential care services, are aware of the importance of regular site reviews and safety planning to minimise the opportunities of harmful sexual behaviour. They must also respond effectively if an incident takes place. It is unlikely that harmful sexual behaviours can ever be entirely prevented but increasing the capacity of communities to be able to identify and effectively respond to harmful sexual behaviour is essential to support children's safety and wellbeing.

References

Atkinson, J 2002, *Trauma trails, re-creating songlines: The intergenerational effects of trauma in Indigenous Australia*, Spinifex Press, North Melbourne.

Auster, CJ & Mansbach, CS 2012, 'The gender marketing of toys: An analysis of color and type of toy on the Disney store website', *Sex Roles*, no. 67, pp. 375–388, <https://doi.org/10.1007/s11199-012-0177-8>.

Australian Bureau of Statistics 2018, *Household use of information technology, Australia, 2016–17*, Catalogue Number 8146.0, ABS, North Melbourne.

Australian Childhood Foundation 2010, *Making space for learning: Trauma informed practice in schools*, Australian Childhood Foundation, Richmond, viewed 20 January 2019, <www.childhood.org.au/for-professionals/resources>.

Australian Institute of Family Studies 2017, *Child Protection Australia 2016–2017*, Canberra, <www.aihw.gov.au/getmedia/66c7c364-592a-458c-9ab0-f90022 e25368/aihw-cws-63.pdf.aspx?inline=true>.

Australian Institute of Health and Welfare 2019, *Child protection Australia: 2017–18*, Child Welfare Series, no. 70, Catalogue Number CWS 65, AIHW, Canberra.

Bowes, J & Hayes, A 2004, 'Contexts and consequences: Impacts on children, families and communities', in J Bowes (ed), *Children families and communities*, Oxford University Press, Oxford.

Briggs, F 2012, *Child protection: The essential guide for teachers and professionals whose work involves children*, Jojo Publishing, Docklands, Victoria.

Briggs, F with McVeity, M 2000, *Teaching children to protect themselves*, Allen & Unwin, Sydney.

Bronfenbrenner, U 1979, *The ecology of human development*, Harvard University Press, Cambridge, MA.

Bronfenbrenner, U 2005, *Making human beings human: Biological perspectives on human development*, Sage Publications, London.

Burton, DL 2000, 'Were adolescent sexual offenders children with sexual behavior problems?' *Sex Abuse*, vol. 12, pp. 37–48, <https://doi.org/10.1023/A:1009511 804302>.

Cradock, A, O'Donnell, E, Benjamin, S, Walker, E & Slining, M 2010, 'A review of state regulations to promote physical activity and safety on playgrounds in child care centers and family child care homes', *Journal of Physical Activity and Health*, vol. 7, no. 1, pp. S108–S119, <https://doi.org/10.1123/jpah.7.s1.s108>.

Department for Education 2019a, *Keeping safe: Child protection curriculum*, Department for Education, Adelaide.

Department for Education 2019b, *Responding to problem sexual behaviours in children and young people: Guidelines for care and education staff*, Department for Education, Adelaide.

Donisch, K, Bray, C & Gewirtz, A 2016, 'Child welfare, juvenile justice, mental health, and education providers' conceptualizations of trauma-informed practice', *Child Maltreatment*, vol. 21 no. 2, pp. 125–134, <https://doi.org/10.1177/1077559516633304>.

Elkovitch, N, Latzman, RD, Hansen, DJ, & Flood, MF 2009, 'Understanding child sexual behavior problems: A developmental psychopathology framework', *Clinical Psychology Review*, vol. 29, no. 7, pp. 586–598.

Elliott, A & Carnes, C 2001, 'Reactions of nonoffending parents to the sexual abuse of their child: A review of the literature', *Child Maltreatment*, vol. 6, no. 4, pp. 314–331.

Evertsz, J & Kirsner, J 2003, *Issues for intellectually disabled children with problem sexual behaviours: Literature review and research report*, Australian Childhood Foundation, Melbourne.

Evertsz, J & Miller, R 2012, *Children with problem sexual behaviours and their families: Best interests case practice model: Specialist practice resource*, Department of Human Services, Melbourne.

Ey, L 2017, 'Sexualised media and critical media literacy: A review of the Australian and the United States primary school curriculum frameworks', *Journal of Curriculum Perspectives*, vol. 37, no. 1, pp. 109–119, <https://doi.org/10.1007/s41297-016-0006-2>.

Ey, L & Cupit, CG 2013, 'Primary school children's imitation of sexualised music videos and artists', *Children Australia*, vol. 38, no. 3, pp. 115–123.

Ey, L, McInnes, E & Rigney, L 2017, 'Educators' understanding of young children's typical and problematic sexual behaviour and their training in this area', *Sex Education*, July, <https://doi.org/10.1080/14681811.2017.1357030>.

Families, Housing, Community Services and Indigenous Affairs Department (FHCSIA) 2010, *Closing the gap: Prime minister's report*, Department of Families, Housing, Community Services and Indigenous Affairs, Canberra.

Fivush, R 1991, 'Gender and emotion in mother-child conversations about the past', *Journal of Narrative and Life History*, vol. 1, no. 4, pp. 325–341, <https://doi.org/10.1075/jnlh.1.4.04gen>.

Flood, M 2007, 'Exposure to pornography among youth in Australia', *Journal of Sociology*, vol. 43, no. 1, pp. 45–60, <https://doi.org/10.1177/1440783307073934>.

Griffore, R & Phenice, L 2016, 'Proximal processes and causality in human development', *European Journal of Educational and Development Psychology*, vol. 4, no. 1, pp. 10–16.

Challenges and prevention strategies 113

Internet Industry Association 2008, *Internet industry code of practice content services code for industry co-regulation in the area of content services* (Pursuant to the Requirements of Schedule 7 of the Broadcasting Services Act 1992 as amended), Internet Industry Association.

Krone, T & Smith, RG 2017, 'Trajectories in online child sexual exploitation offending in Australia', *Trends and issues in crime and criminal justice*, no. 524, Australian Institute of Criminology, Canberra.

Lynch, M & Cicchetti, D 1998, 'An ecological-transactional analysis of children and contexts: The longitudinal interplay among child maltreatment, community violence, and children's symptomatology', *Development and Psychopathology*, vol. 10, no. 2, pp. 235–57, <https://doi.org/10.1017/S095457949800159>.

McHale, SM, Dotterer, A & Kim, JY 2009, 'An ecological perspective on the media and youth development', *American Behavioral Scientist*, vol. 52, no. 8, pp. 1186–1203, <https://doi.org/10.1177/0002764209331541>.

McInnes, E 2014, 'Madness in family law: Mothers' mental health in the Australian family law system', *Psychiatry, Psychology and Law*, vol. 21, no. 1, pp. 78–91, <https://doi.org/10.1080/13218719.2013.774688>.

McInnes, E 2015, 'A feminist perspective: System responses to Australian mothers exiting an abusive relationship', in M Taylor, JA Pooley & RS Taylor (eds), *Overcoming domestic violence: Creating a dialogue round vulnerable populations*, Nova Science Publishers, New York.

McInnes, E & Diamond, A 2011, 'Child and family centres: How effective?', in K Brettig & M Sims (eds), *Building integrated communities for children, their families and communities*, Cambridge Scholars Publishing, Newcastle on Tyne.

Meiksans, J, Bromfield, L & Ey, L 2017, *A continuum of responses for harmful sexual behaviours*, Perth, <www.ccyp.wa.gov.au/media/2973/a-continuum-of-responses-for-harmful-sexual-behaviours-australian-centre-for-child-protection-april-2018.pdf>.

Mesman, GR, Harper, SL, Edge, NA, Brandt, TW & Pemberton, JL 2019, 'Problematic sexual behaviour in children', *Journal of Pediatric Health Care*, vol. 33, no. 3, pp. 323–331, <https://doi.org/10.1016/j.pedhc.2018.11.002>.

O'Brien, W 2008, *Problem sexual behaviour in children: A review of the literature*, Australian Crime Commission, Canberra.

Parliament of South Australia 2019, *Aboriginal lands parliamentary standing committee report on the key issues raised during its visit to the Aṉangu Pitjantjatjara Yankunytjatjara lands, 7–9 May 2019*, Adelaide.

Peterson, C 2010, *Looking forward through the lifespan: Developmental psychology*, 5th edn, Pearson, Frenchs Forest, Australia.

Pintello, D & Zuravin, S 2001, 'Intrafamilial child sexual abuse: Predictors of post-disclosure maternal belief and protective action,' *Child Maltreatment*, vol. 6, no. 4, pp. 344–352.

Rosa, E & Tudge, J 2013, 'Urie Bronfenbrenner's theory of human development: Its evolution from ecology to bioecology', *Journal of Family Theory Review*, vol. 5, no. 4, pp. 243–258.

Rothbart, MK 2007, 'Temperament, development and personality', *Current Directions in psychological science*, vol. 16, no. 4, pp. 207–212.

Rowley, T & Edwards, J 2007, *Everybody's got a bottom*, Family Planning Queensland, Brisbane.

Smith, TJ, Lindsey, RA, Bohora, S & Silovsky, JS 2019, 'Predictors of intrusive sexual behaviors in preschool-aged children', *The Journal of Sex Research*, vol. 56, no. 2, pp. 229–238.

Streeck-Fischer, A & van der Kolk, B 2000, 'Down will come baby, cradle and all: Diagnostic and therapeutic implications of chronic trauma on child development', *Australian and New Zealand Journal of Psychiatry*, vol. 34, no. 6, pp. 903–918.

Webster, K, Diemer, K, Honey, N, Mannix, S, Mickle, J, Morgan, J, Parkes, A, Politoff, V, Powell, A, Stubbs, J & Ward, A 2019, *Australians' attitudes to violence against women and gender equality: Findings from the 2017 national community attitudes survey towards violence against women survey*, ANROWS, NSW.

10 Conclusion

Introduction

This chapter draws together the key learnings about harmful sexual behaviour and some of the grave implications if we fail to collectively reduce and manage its incidence in care and education sites, as well as in wider society. The need for children's protection from maltreatment, trauma, and exposures to influences such as pornography and online exploitation is likely to remain a continuing challenge, as is the need for professionals who can recognise and respond effectively to the needs of children and their families.

The many challenges arising from children's harmful sexual behaviour have informed the structure of this book as a brief guide to the issue. This chapter begins with a review of some of the factors which have given rise to increased attention to the issue before turning to the implications for action to improve responses to harmful sexual behaviours. The chapter concludes with a review of the central learnings arising from the content of preceding chapters.

Harmful sexual behaviour has increasingly been recognised as an issue of concern in Australia and countries around the world. This raised awareness in Australia can be attributed to a range of factors, including:

- increased numbers of children experiencing maltreatment (AIHW 2019);
- increased numbers of children attending formal child care services (ABS 2017);
- rapid growth in pornography and child exploitation material online (Maley 2019);
- numerous state government inquiries into child sexual abuse and child protection systems:
  - South Australia (Layton 2003; Mullighan 2008; Debelle 2013; Nyland 2016);

- Western Australia (Gordon, Hallahan, & Henry 2002);
- Northern Territory (Wild & Anderson 2007);
- Tasmania (O'Halloran 2011);
- Queensland (Forde 1999; Carmody 2013);
- New South Wales (NSW Legislative Council 2017); and
- Victoria (Victoria Parliament 2013).

- federal government inquiries:
  - *Lost Innocence* inquiry into child migration (Senate Community Affairs Reference Committee 2001);
  - *Forgotten Australians* inquiry into Australians who experienced institutional or out-of-home care as children (Senate Community Affairs Reference Committee 2004);
  - *Royal Commission into Institutional Responses to Child Sexual Abuse* (Royal Commission into Institutional Responses to Child Sexual Abuse 2017a).

The following sections briefly review these factors and the developing awareness of the incidence of harmful sexual behaviours, before addressing some of the key learnings around necessary action to reduce and prevent harmful sexual behaviours.

Increased numbers of children experiencing maltreatment

The Australian Institute of Health and Welfare's *Child protection 2017–18* (2019) identifies that approximately 159,000 children received child protection services in the form of either an investigation, care and protection order, or out-of-home placement. A total of 72% of these children had previously received child protection services. Indigenous children received child protection services at eight times the rate of non-Indigenous children. The rate of receipt of child protection services has increased from 7.2 to 8.5 for children who were the subject of substantiated abuse in the five years from 2013–14 to 2017–18. Research has made clear that complex trauma involving multiple forms of child maltreatment over time is a strong contributor to the development of harmful sexual behaviours (Elkovitch, Latzman, Hansen, & Flood 2009; Kambouropoulos 2005; Mesman, Harper, Edge, Brandt, & Pemberton 2019). The prevalence of family violence and all forms of child maltreatment impacts the proportion of children who are vulnerable to developing harmful sexual behaviours.

Grant et al. (2009) identify that sexual abuse of children by other children, or adolescents, accounts for between 40–90% of sexual abuse of children, with siblings being responsible for a significant proportion of this behaviour. They note that, like children with harmful sexual behaviour, adolescents who engaged in harmful sexual behaviours with other children often had a history of developmental trauma arising from physical victimisation, variously involving physical and sexual abuse and exposure to family violence. Burton (2000) and Grant et al. (2009) identify the risk of a trajectory of harmful sexual behaviour into adolescent harmful sexual behaviours without effective intervention. Both boys and girls are vulnerable to repeated sexual exploitation by multiple offenders (Briggs 2012); however, males are more likely to become criminalised if harmful sexual behaviours persist (Burton 2000). Girls remain highly vulnerable to sexual exploitation, and many who work in the sex trade report past experiences of child sexual abuse (Abramovich 2005).

Reducing rates of all forms of child maltreatment and family violence is thus critical to reducing the number of children vulnerable to developing harmful sexual behaviour.

Increased numbers of children attending formal child care

Children are increasingly likely to attend a formal child care service. The proportion of children aged 0–12 attending formal care services has risen from 9% in 1996 to 19% in 2017 (ABS 2017). The growth in demand for formal child care has accompanied women's rising workforce participation in Australia and extended young children's structured participation in public spaces outside their home. This means that more children are exposed to other children outside their family networks in care settings. Sexualised behaviour which may have previously taken place behind closed doors is now visible to educators and carers trained in child development and child abuse indicators. They are also professionally obligated to make a report to child protection services if they reasonably suspect child abuse or harmful sexual behaviour.

Major employers of care and education staff, such as the South Australian Department for Education (2019b), have developed guidelines for staff to ensure that they have resources to identify and respond to harmful sexual behaviour. Children attending such services may be impacted by witnessing behaviour such as genital exposure, masturbation, or sexual interactions with other children, or may be directly accosted to engage in sexual activity, including genital touching, oral sex, and penetration.

Educators are the professionals responsible for the ongoing work of supporting children's learning and wellbeing and are also responsible for ensuring that families have the information they need when incidents involving harmful sexual behaviour occur. It is therefore vital that educators and carers have the training and information they need to feel prepared and supported to act effectively in response to harmful sexual behaviour.

Public inquiries into child protection systems and child sexual abuse

Public inquiries into child protection issues serve to place a focus on the dimensions of child abuse as a public health and criminal justice issue.

State public inquiries into child abuse and child protection

It is critical that state government child protection systems are effective in supporting children's safety and ensuring access to therapeutic intervention, which will help reduce the number of children exposed to maltreatment that increases their risk of developing harmful sexual behaviour. Investigations of state child protection services over the previous two decades have revealed endemic problems of overwhelming demand, budget blowouts, difficulties recruiting and retaining appropriately trained staff and foster carers, abuse of children in out-of-home care by adults and other children, and a tendency within institutions to place the interests of the organisation ahead of children's needs.

South Australia has conducted four major investigations into child sexual abuse and child protection in the past two decades. In 2003, Robyn Layton QC provided a comprehensive analysis of the state child protection system, making recommendations to overhaul responses to child abuse reports, system structures, legal processes, and the education and training of professionals (Layton 2003). The Layton Report did not specifically consider the issue of harmful sexual behaviour but rather focused on responses to child sexual abuse by adults.

The issues of sexual abuse and deaths of children living in state care were examined in a Commission of Inquiry from 2004 to 2008, which examined cases stretching back four decades (Mullighan 2008). The inquiry took evidence from 792 victims (406 males and 386 females), with 1,592 allegations against 1,733 alleged perpetrators. The allegations nominated perpetrators including staff, people the child was taken to visit, visitors to care sites, and other older children in care. The inquiry made 54 recommendations to improve the education and training of professionals responding to child sexual abuse; to educate children in protective behaviours; to improve response processes and record-keeping; and to improve support structures for children living in alternative care (Mullighan 2008). Although the issue of child-child sexual behaviour was raised by victims, it was not a specific focus of recommendations.

Conclusion 119

In 2012, the Debelle Royal Commission was established to investigate processes surrounding responses to the sexual abuse of a child attending an out-of-school-hours care service at a state government school in 2011. The Debelle Report, released in 2013, included a survey of sexual offending in schools between 2009 and 2012, identifying 75 instances of sexual misconduct by adults. Sexual misconduct or harmful sexual behaviours among children were not referenced in the report (Debelle 2013). The focus of recommended changes related to processes for informing parents in the school community when a child was affected by adult sexual offending. Despite this gap, the report highlighted the school and education department responsibilities for appropriate communication with the school community about concerning sexual behaviour, which is also relevant in cases in which a child's harmful sexual behaviours have affected other children attending the site.

A royal commission into the South Australian child protection system was established in 2014 and reported in 2016 (Nyland 2016). The catalyst for the inquiry was the arrest of a child protection worker, Shannon McCoole, who was later convicted of sexually abusing young children in his care and posting images to a global network (Nyland 2016). McCoole had been reported by a colleague who suspected he had abused a child in his care. She was dismissed and he was promoted. McCoole's offending was eventually identified by international police tracking images on a child exploitation network which he hosted (Lee 2019). He was jailed for 35 years. The case highlighted the challenges facing an overburdened child protection system which was struggling to respond to child abuse reports and to recruit and retain qualified staff. Nyland noted that in 2014–15, 61% of child protection notifications that were assessed as requiring a response were closed without any action being taken (2016, p. xvi). The inquiry identified that 70% of the child protection budget was used to fund alternative care, with prevention and early intervention actions being severely financially restricted (2016, p. xiv). The report noted that 'one of the most striking observations made by the Commission is the yawning gap between policy requirements and day-to-day practice in many areas' (2016, p. xiv). Nyland's recommendations included the formation of a dedicated child protection department; the establishment of a family support service pathway for matters that did not reach a statutory intervention threshold; better expert assessments; more education in child sexual abuse dynamics; improvements in recruitment screening and in the quality of care placements; supervision; and service delivery. Although the Nyland inquiry focus on the child protection system did not specifically include children's harmful sexual behaviour, the emphasis on the quality of alternative care provisions and children's access to therapy do go some way to addressing the risks of harmful sexual behaviours once a report is made to child protection services.

The cumulative effect of the four inquiries in two decades into responses to child sexual abuse in South Australia cannot be easily measured. However, the repeated failures of the child protection system were laid bare in the evidence collected. Vigilant intervention; appropriate, timely responses by government departments; and access to therapeutic services for child victims have been repeatedly demonstrated as vital in South Australia and in similar public inquiries in other state jurisdictions.

The New South Wales Legislative Council conducted an inquiry into child protection in that state, reporting in 2017 that in 2015–16 the system received almost 200,000 reports of abuse and that around 20,000 children in that state lived in alternative care, a number which had doubled in the past decade. The report's authors described the content as 'bitter reading' (2017, p. ix) in relation to the ability of the Department of Family and Community services 'to fully comprehend, plan and execute its mandate'.

The Queensland government's Forde inquiry (1999) examined abuse of children in Queensland institutions from 1911 to 1999, identifying extensive individual and systemic abuses of children living in orphanages and detention centres. In 2013, the state's child protection system was again examined (Carmody 2013, p. xi), identifying three main causes of systemic failure: too little money spent on early intervention to support vulnerable families; a widespread risk-averse culture that focused too heavily on coercive instead of supportive strategies and overreacted to (or overcompensated for) hostile media and community scrutiny; and, linked with this, a tendency from all parts of society to shift responsibility onto Child Safety.

The Tasmanian inquiry (O'Halloran 2011) made similar findings about that state's child protection system. These inquiries did not raise the issue of child-child harmful sexual behaviours, but rather that the enduring failure of child protection systems to effectively protect children provided the basis for intergenerational cycles of risks of child maltreatment.

The Gordon inquiry in Western Australia, *Putting the picture together: Inquiry into response by government agencies to complaints of family violence and child abuse in Aboriginal communities* (Gordon et al. 2002), examined government responses to reports of family violence and child abuse in Aboriginal communities. The inquiry was called following a child's death in a case with extensive involvement with state services. The inquiry concluded that there were ongoing cultural issues adversely affecting provision of police and child protection services to Aboriginal communities. In the Northern Territory, the *Little children are sacred* report (Wild & Anderson 2007) emerged from an inquiry into 'the extent, nature and factors contributing to the sexual abuse of Aboriginal children' (Wild & Anderson 2007 p. 41). This report acknowledged the issue of child-child harmful sexual behaviour:

> The Inquiry is further concerned that:
> - sometimes sex between children may contain an element of inequality and coercion that children may be incapable of effectively dealing with;
> - unchecked sexualised youth are more vulnerable to becoming victims or offenders of sexual abuse.
>
> Sex between children was a primary cause of widespread concern in all communities that the Inquiry visited.
> (Wild & Anderson 2007, p. 65)

The Northern Territory and Western Australian reports confirm that Aboriginal and Torres Strait Islander peoples of Australia continue to be both overrepresented in child protection systems and are often adversely impacted by them. The Wild and Anderson (2007) report's focus on the issue of sexualisation of children highlights the enduring traumatisation and sexual exploitation of Australia's First Nation peoples (Atkinson 2002).

The Victorian Parliament Family and Community Development Committee Inquiry into the Handling of Child Abuse by Religious and other Non-Government Organisations made its report, *Betrayal of trust*, in 2013. The report identified the tendency for organisations to be 'motivated by self-interest and the protection of the organisation' (p. xxx). These findings were to be reinforced on a national scale by a federal Royal Commission.

Federal public inquiries relating to child abuse issues

Relevant federal government inquiries have variously examined the experiences of children in care institutions. These inquiries arose from state actions relating to child protection, juvenile justice, and child migration to Australia and have identified pervasive problems of child sexual abuse by adults and child-child harmful sexual behaviours.

The *Lost innocence* report of the Senate Community Affairs Reference Committee (2001) examined the experiences and continuing needs of people who were sent to Australia as children from the United Kingdom. It identified the pervasive abuse of these children living in care institutions and their lifelong suffering from the abuse. The *Forgotten Australians* inquiry of the Senate Community Affairs Reference Committee (2004) inquired into experiences of more than half a million Australians who had been placed in forms of out-of-home care arising from poverty, abuse, juvenile crime, parental death or abandonment, or being born to an unmarried mother. Again, key identified issues were the pervasive and persistent abuse of children in care, the lack of support services, and the long-term impacts:

> A lifelong inability to initiate and maintain stable, loving relationships was described by many care leavers who have undergone multiple relationships and failed marriages. Many cannot form trust in relationships and remain loners, never marrying or living an isolated existence.
> (Senate Community Affairs Reference Committee 2004, p. xv)

The continuing problem of the failure of religious and secular care and education institutions to recognise and reform their responses to complainants of child abuse, as identified in Victoria's *Betrayal of trust* report in 2013, gave rise to Australia's Royal Commission into Institutional Responses to Child Sexual Abuse. This commenced in 2013 and provided its final report in 2017, drawing national attention to the problem of child sexual abuse and the ways in which organisations have responded. Approximately 16,000 people contacted the Commission and made reports involving more than 4,000 organisations. The Commission's final report drew on the experiences of 6,875 survivors, of whom more than 64% were male (Royal Commission into Institutional Responses to Child Sexual Abuse 2017a). More than 93% of identified abusers were male, and approximately 16% of abusers were aged under 18. A total of 62% of children who engaged in sexually harmful behaviour with other children were males, and 38% were females (Royal Commission into Institutional Responses to Child Sexual Abuse 2017, p. 10). The Commission identified that, in addition to physical and sexual abuse, exposures to family violence, sexualised imagery and behaviour, institutional contexts of violence, and coercion also created risks of harmful sexual behaviour by children and young people. They noted the following characteristics of such institutions:

- encouragement of sexualised behaviours;
- physical and emotional abuse and neglect;
- bullying and initiation rituals;
- hierarchical structures where children held power over other children;
- lack of supervision of children;

- lack of understanding of children's sexual development and of harmful sexual behaviours; and
- inadequate provision of sex education to support healthy behaviours.

(Royal Commission into Institutional Responses to Child Sexual Abuse 2017b, p. 11)

The Commission identified that at the time of making its report, state and territory governments lacked a nationally consistent approach to preventing, identifying, and responding to children with harmful sexual behaviours. The Commission recommended primary prevention through the education of adults and children in developmentally appropriate sexual behaviours, taking into account the age, gender, culture, and disability status of different groups. In cases in which harmful sexual behaviours occurred, institutions and organisations needed clear protocols for responses to children and families, communications, and documentation of events. Children involved in instances of harmful sexual behaviour required access to therapeutic services involving trauma-informed expert assessment of each child's context and needs. However, the Commission was informed of serious gaps and inconsistencies in the services provided, such that children could easily miss out on the care they needed, especially in rural and remote areas of Australia (Royal Commission into Institutional Responses to Child Sexual Abuse 2017b, pp. 11–16). The Royal Commission into Institutional Responses in Child Sexual Abuse generated much greater social awareness of the scale of child sexual abuse in Australia and the depth and duration of harm caused to victims and survivors, regardless of whether the behaviour was enacted by an adult or another child. The Commission's attention to children's harmful sexual behaviours also drew attention to the significance of such behaviours as a part of the overall problem of child sexual abuse.

Rapid growth in pornography and child exploitation material online

The rise of digital technologies and the accompanying growth in the online circulation of pornography and child exploitation material has given rise to new dimensions of threats to children. Along with the online risks of sexting and cyber-bullying, children can be targeted by adults online for grooming and sexual abuse or recruited into the production of child exploitation material, as in the case of Shannon McCoole, referred to earlier. A newspaper report in December 2019 (Maley 2019) cited Australian Federal Police Commissioner Reece Kershaw, stating that increasingly violent online child abuse material was proliferating on the 'dark web' and that police were increasingly concerned about the link between online child pornography and 'contact offending' against children in the real world. The police commissioner commented that 'the proliferation of child abuse material online suggested child sexual abuse remained significantly underreported and misunderstood'. Krone and Smith's (2017) research found the strongest links to contact offending involved people who produced and uploaded child exploitation material to networks. The primary methods of discovery of children used in the production of child exploitation material involve police investigation of images already online (Westlake, Bouchard, Frank, & Fraser 2012). The images provide digital evidence which does not rely on the contested testimony of individuals but relies on the identification of offenders, the sites of the offending, and the children who are being used. Finding and infiltrating online networks sharing illegal child exploitation material requires detecting such material in encrypted and 'dark web' communications.

Production of child exploitation material involving infants and very young children has the advantage for perpetrators that they are relatively easily controlled and lack the knowledge and verbal ability to tell anyone what has happened to them (Briggs 2012). Young children and children with intellectual and communication disabilities cannot give evidence as witnesses in any criminal proceedings (Layton 2003). With high financial gains to be made in child sex trafficking and in producing and circulating digital imagery of child exploitation, young children can be subject to sexual abuse by adults and made to perform sexual acts on each other, thereby establishing some of the identified risk factors for harmful sexual behaviour from a very young age, with repeated events and multiple offenders (Smith, Lindsey, Bohora, & Silovsky 2019). Perpetrators gain access to children by removing, grooming, or controlling their potential protectors and may also engage in building networks with other offenders to enable, conceal, and circulate child exploitation activity (Briggs 2012; Krone & Smith 2017).

What's to be done?

This book has sought to provide insight and guidance from research and practice knowledge regarding children with harmful sexual behaviour. This section reviews the key learnings derived from the preceding chapters. Following the introductory Chapter 1, Chapter 2 addresses the need for understanding children's age-appropriate sexual development in order to discern the behaviours that fall outside an age-appropriate range and require intervention and management to contain and minimise harm to

Conclusion 125

the child and to others who may be affected. The chapter provides guidance regarding the language and definitions of sexual behaviour which distinguish between developmentally appropriate, concerning, and harmful behaviours.

Chapter 3 presents the rising prevalence of children with harmful sexual behaviours across the globe and across the social spectrum and highlights the gaps in current data, indicating that the number of children engaging in harmful sexual behaviour is likely to be greater than the research suggests. The increasing prevalence of children's harmful sexual behaviour requires a new training and education paradigm in child protection that explicitly engages with child-child sexual behaviour. Parents, educators, and other professionals engaging with children need to be able to identify and respond appropriately to harmful sexual behaviour.

Chapter 4 identifies some of the consequences for children which arise from incidents of harmful sexual behaviour, which can result in serious short-term and longer-term impacts for affected children. Children displaying sexual behaviours may be forced to leave the care or education site and be restricted in their attendance. They are also vulnerable to being stigmatised, further impacting their development. Without appropriate therapeutic support and behaviour change, they may continue to enact harmful sexual behaviour and experience increased risk of disrupted education and contact with the justice system as they get older. Children and families affected by the harmful sexual behaviour of others also require therapeutic care to recover from their experiences. The Royal Commission into Institutional Responses to Child Sexual Abuse (2017b) identified that there are still significant gaps in reliable and timely access to services which can assist children with harmful sexual behaviours, particularly for children with intellectual disabilities and children living in rural and remote areas of Australia. The availability of suitable services for all children and families is an urgent issue if we are to effectively address harmful sexual behaviours. Children from families with diverse language and cultural backgrounds, those with disabilities, and those living in non-metropolitan areas require accessible quality services equal to those living in major centres. The affordances of virtual service delivery may overcome challenges of distance; however, there is a need to boost the size of the workforce with trauma-informed specialist skills to engage children and their families. It is important that educators recognise the impacts for all children involved and respond to the behaviour rather than labelling the child.

The factors contributing to the risks of children displaying harmful sexual behaviours are discussed in Chapter 5. Family violence, child maltreatment, and exposure to sexualised conduct and imagery are ubiquitous and intractable social issues contributing to the development of harmful

126 Conclusion

sexual behaviour. The raised public awareness of the significant impacts of maltreatment and complex trauma on children's development presents opportunities for improving support and education for families with young children, as well as for the professionals who work with them. Research tracing the cumulative impacts of trauma on children's neurodevelopment has demonstrated that children growing up in highly stressful environments of fear and physical harm adapt to survival modes of dissociation or hyperarousal, both of which hamper normal learning and development (Perry 2005; Streeck-Fischer & van der Kolk 2000). In contrast to previous beliefs that young children cannot remember trauma and therefore are unharmed by it, researchers now understand that early experiences imprint and inform children's subsequent interactions with their environment (Perry 2005). Exposure to coercive violence and sexual abuse shape a blueprint for survival-driven behaviour which can be maladaptive outside such contexts. All professionals who work with children and families need to understand the impacts of trauma on development and undergo training in trauma-informed practice with children and adults. The impacts of trauma can be reduced by establishing safety and working with those affected to develop a sense of control over their environment, providing developmentally appropriate opportunities for choice and consistent success (Perry 2005; Streeck-Fischer & van der Kolk 2000). Reducing rates of family violence and child maltreatment, whilst strengthening families' capacities to meet children's needs, are necessary strategies to stem the flow of traumatised children vulnerable to developing harmful sexual behaviour.

Chapter 6 focuses on the legal dimensions of Australia's responses to child sexual abuse and to children's harmful sexual behaviour. The difficulty of detecting and successfully prosecuting child sexual abuse remains a feature of a legal system designed by adults, for adults. Children below the age of 10 who exhibit harmful sexual behaviour may progress into the juvenile justice system if their behaviour persists. The public inquiries into child protection systems and legal responses to child sexual abuse have collectively provided many insights into the problems and challenges of preventing child maltreatment and recommendations for reform. These have variously resulted in the introduction of children's commissioners; guidelines for child safe organisations; employment and volunteer screening for those working with children; changes to procedures for training educators, social workers, and health professionals in identifying and responding to child abuse; changes to criminal prosecution processes to improve access to justice for child victims; and structural improvements in child protection. Despite these measures, enormous challenges remain.

Conclusion 127

The needs of educators and carers in identifying and responding to harmful sexual behaviours is discussed in Chapter 7. Australia's universal education system means that it is the main service available to children on a regular basis. Educators and carers have thus come to be an important frontline in detecting and reporting suspected child maltreatment, second only to police as the main profession making child protection notifications resulting in investigations (AIHW 2019, p. 22). Australian educators report observing children's harmful sexual behaviours in their care and educator settings (Ey & McInnes 2018) and want training in how to respond to these behaviours (Ey, McInnes & Rigney 2017). Educators want to be able to access information and support on demand in their workplace as incidents arise, as well as structured access to training and clear lines of support from site leadership (McInnes & Ey 2019). Managing children's harmful sexual behaviours is often experienced by educators as stressful and distressing (McInnes & Ey 2019). Training, clear guidelines and processes, access to therapeutic services, as well as leadership support are necessary to ensure that educators feel prepared to respond effectively.

Chapter 8 examines the work of educators and carers in restoring and maintaining safety for children when an incident occurs. Educators and carers spend the most regular time with children after families, and thus ideally provide day-to-day opportunities for affected children to experience a safe environment, to learn positive ways of relating to others, and to develop their sense of identity and belonging. Children with harmful sexual behaviours cannot develop their social and emotional skills without opportunities to interact with a community of peers, and again it falls to educators to ensure that these behaviours do not put the child or other children at risk. Educators' approaches to teaching, their relationships with children, their classroom management strategies, and their communication practices all affect the learning experiences of children who have undergone chronic stress and trauma (McInnes, Whitington, Diamond, & Neill 2020; Perry 2020). The role of educators and carers in child abuse prevention, identification, and response needs to be acknowledged and supported on a national basis by ongoing public investment in education and training in supporting traumatised children, and through partnerships with health and therapeutic services for families and children.

The role of prevention and the challenges of reducing harmful sexual behaviours are addressed in Chapter 9. The ecological approach to analysing and addressing factors impacting children's behaviour requires attention to the child's individual needs as well as the contexts of families and communities in which children grow and develop. Reducing child maltreatment is a complex problem. An ecological approach to reducing child maltreatment would take into account each child's individual needs and support parents' knowledge and capacity. It would enable access to quality health services, child care, and education services alongside a functional labour market, housing market, and welfare system, ensuring that families are able to receive sufficient income to remain housed, put food on the table, and enable their participation in safe communities (Lynch & Cicchetti 1998). In economies with insecure work, high unemployment, unaffordable housing, and welfare payments well below the poverty line, parents experiencing social disadvantage have reduced options to improve their circumstances and are often forced to live in neighbourhoods with higher crime rates and fewer community services. Education and support for parents needs to be universally provided and much more widely accessible as a primary, secondary, and tertiary prevention measure. All parents can benefit from information about child health and development, such as replacing physical punishments with alternative ways of supporting children's pro-social behaviour. They would also benefit from education in ways to reduce and manage risks to children's safety (Chen & Chan 2016).

Reducing child maltreatment also requires reducing domestic and family violence and tackling sexual violence and abuse more effectively. Hooker, Kaspiew, and Taft (2016) identify that an estimated one third of Australian parents in the general community experience domestic and family violence. They recommend that mothers be supported to achieve safety with their children in preference to the current, dominant policy approach of reporting domestic and family violence to child protection services, which may result in children being secondarily traumatised by being removed to alternative care. Domestic and family violence and community legal services in Australia have been subjected to reduced levels of government funding (Murphy 2016) as victimisation rates remain high. Without access to safe housing and adequate income, mothers and children cannot easily leave violent relationships. Australia's criminal justice and family law systems routinely enable perpetrators of violence and abuse to escape significant consequences for violence and abuse of women and children (McInnes 2015). The intergenerational legacies of child abuse and family violence, along with reduced levels of support for struggling families, indicate a likely rise in rates of child maltreatment and consequent vulnerability to harmful sexual behaviour.

Whilst there is a need to reduce domestic and family violence and child maltreatment, and to develop parenting skills and social support resources, the rise of the internet has dramatically increased risks to children through exposure to sexual content and sexual exploitation. The significant rise in sexualised media and internet pornography sites has resulted in children being exposed to sexual material. Furthermore, the digital environment remains a frontier where regulators and lawmakers trail well behind

Conclusion 129

those who use the internet to stalk and groom children, to produce and consume child exploitation material, to facilitate child sex trafficking, and to abuse children on demand using live-streaming technology (Schell, Vargas, Patrick, Hung, & Rueda 2007). Encryption, virtual private networks, and the 'dark web' cross international boundaries, enabling offenders to exploit children for global consumption in jurisdictions with less policing. As with adult pornography, child exploitation material has become increasingly abusive. 'Child hurtcore porn' is a term coined to describe content which emphasises torture and degradation involving pre-adolescent children, including infants less than 2 years old (Johnston & Bucci 2015; Schell et al. 2007). The exponential rise in demand for child exploitation material is a key challenge to reducing and preventing child sexual abuse. A news report from the United States (Mojica 2017) stated that the National Center for Missing and Exploited Children (NCMEC) estimated that more than 26 million sexual abuse images and videos were received by their analysts in 2015. More than 10,500 victims depicted in child exploitation material had been identified by police since 2002. The article reported that one website on the dark web was shown to have 200,000 registered users and that 100,000 individuals had accessed the site over 12 days. The scale of the child exploitation problem presents a daunting challenge to the task of reducing and preventing child sexual abuse and the consequent incidence of harmful sexual behaviours.

The futures of children who display harmful sexual behaviour will vary according to the circumstances and events that have contributed to the behaviour, as well as the responses of those responsible for identifying and managing the behaviour. Proactive intervention through a trauma-informed lens is vital to the futures of affected children and their families, as well as to the wider society, to protect future generations. Harmful sexual behaviours are likely to continue. They demand a continuous and persistent process of strategic national and state government response across the education, social work, health, and legal professions.

References

Abramovich, E 2005, 'Childhood sexual abuse as a risk factor for subsequent involvement in sex work', *Journal of Psychology & Human Sexuality*, vol. 17, nos. 1–2, pp. 131–146, <https://doi.org/10.1300/J056v17n01_08>.

Atkinson, J 2002, *Trauma trails, re-creating songlines: The intergenerational effects of trauma in Indigenous Australia*, Spinifex Press, North Melbourne.

Australian Bureau of Statistics 2017, *Childhood Education and Care*, Catalogue Number 4402.0, Australian Bureau of Statistics, Canberra.

Australian Institute of Health and Welfare 2019, *Child protection Australia 2017–2018*, Australian Institute of Health and Welfare, Canberra, <www.aihw.gov.au/getmedia/e551a2bc-9149-4625-83c0-7bf1523c3793/aihw-cws-65.pdf.aspx?inline=true>.

Briggs, F 2012, *Child Protection: The essential guide for teachers and professionals whose work involves children*, Jojo Publishing, Docklands, Victoria.

Burton, DL 2000, 'Were adolescent sexual offenders children with sexual behavior problems?', *Sex Abuse*, vol. 12, pp. 37–48, <https://doi.org/10.1023/A:1009511804302>.

Carmody, T 2013, *Taking responsibility: A roadmap for Queensland child protection, report of the Queensland child protection commission of inquiry*, Queensland Government, Brisbane.

Chen, M & Chan, KL 2016, 'Effects of parenting programs on child maltreatment prevention: A meta-analysis', *Trauma, Violence & Abuse*, vol. 17, no. 1, pp. 88–104, <https://doi.org/10.1177/1524838014566718>.

Debelle, B 2013, *Independent education inquiry 2012–2013*, SA Government, Adelaide, viewed 27 December 2019, <www.saasso.asn.au/wp-content/uploads/2013/11/DebelleInquiry.pdf>.

Department for Education 2019, *Responding to problem sexual behaviours in children and young people: Guidelines for care and education staff*, Department for Education, Adelaide.

Elkovitch, N, Latzman, RD, Hansen, DJ & Flood, MF 2009, 'Understanding child sexual behavior problems: A developmental psychopathology framework', *Clinical Psychology Review*, vol. 29, no. 7, pp. 586–598.

Ey, L, & McInnes, E 2018, 'Educators' Observations of Children's Display of Problematic Sexual Behaviors in Educational Settings,' *Journal of Child Sexual Abuse*, vol. 27, no. 1, pp. 88–105, doi: 10.1080/10538712.2017.1349855.

Ey, L, McInnes, E & Rigney, L 2017, 'Educators' understanding of young children's typical and problematic sexual behaviour and their training in this area', *Sex education*, vol. 17, no. 6, pp. 682–696, doi: 10.1080/14681811.2017.1357030.

Forde, L 1999, *Report of the commission of inquiry into child abuse in Queensland institutions*, Queensland Government, Brisbane, <www.qld.gov.au/__data/assets/pdf_file/0023/54509/forde-comminquiry.pdf>.

Gordon, S, Hallahan, K & Henry, D 2002, *Putting the picture together: Inquiry into response by government agencies to complaints of family violence and child abuse in Aboriginal communities*, WA Department of Premier and Cabinet, Perth.

Grant, J, Indermaur, D, Thornton, J, Stevens, G, Chamarette, C & Halse, A 2009, 'Intrafamilial adolescent sex offenders: Psychological profile and treatment', *Trends & Issues in Crime and Criminal Justice*, no. 375, Australian Institute of Criminology, Canberra, <https://aic.gov.au/publications/tandi/tandi375>.

Hooker, L, Kaspiew, R & Taft, A 2016, *Domestic and family violence and parenting: Mixed methods insights into impact and support needs: State of knowledge paper*, Australia's National Research Organisation for Women's Safety (ANROWS), <https://d2c0ikyv46o3b1.cloudfront.net/anrows.org.au/s3fs-public/L1.16_1.8%20Parenting.pdf>.

Johnston, C & Bucci, N 2015, 'How Matthew David Graham's 'hurtcore' paedophile habit began on the dark web', *The Age*, September 9, Melbourne, viewed 1 January 2020, <www.theage.com.au/national/victoria/how-matthew-david-grahams-hurtcore-paedophile-habit-began-on-the-dark-web-20150908-gjhz43.html>.

Kambouropoulos, N 2005, 'Understanding the background of children who engage in problem sexual behaviour', in P Staiger (ed), *Children who engage in problem sexual behaviours: Context, characteristics and treatment*, Australian Childhood Foundation and Deakin University, Ringwood, Vic, pp. 9–24.

Krone, T & Smith, RG 2017, 'Trajectories in online child sexual exploitation offending in Australia', *Trends and issues in crime and criminal justice*, no. 524, Australian Institute of Criminology, Canberra.

Layton, R 2003, *Our best investment: A state plan to protect and advance the interests of children*, SA Government, Adelaide, viewed 27 December 2019, <www.childprotection.sa.gov.au/__data/assets/pdf_file/0003/107274/layton-child-protection-review.pdf>.

Lee, S 2019, *Whistleblower claims she was bullied after reporting concerns about paedophile Shannon McCoole*, ABC News, Adelaide.

Lynch, M & Cicchetti, D 1998, 'An ecological-transactional analysis of children and contexts: The longitudinal interplay among child maltreatment, community violence, and children's symptomatology', *Development and Psychopathology*, vol. 10, no. 2, pp. 235–57, <https://doi.org/10.1017/S095457949800159>.

Maley, P 2019, 'Cops warning on "sick" pornography', *The Australian*, December 23.

McInnes, E 2015, 'A feminist perspective: system responses to Australian mothers exiting an abusive relationship', in M Taylor, JA Pooley & RS Taylor (eds), *Overcoming domestic violence: Creating a dialogue round vulnerable populations*, Nova Science Publishers, New York.

McInnes, E & Ey, L 2019, Responding to problematic sexual behaviours of primary school children: Supporting care and education staff, *Sex Education* vol. 20, no. 1, pp. 75–89, <https://doi.org/10.1080/14681811.2019.1621827>.

McInnes, E, Whitington, V, Diamond, A & Neill, B 2020, 'Embedding wellbeing and creating community in classrooms', in K Brettig (ed), *Building stronger communities with children and families*, 2nd edn, Cambridge Scholars Publishing, Newcastle on Tyne, pp. 123–149.

Mesman, GR, Harper, SL, Edge, NA, Brandt, TW & Pemberton, JL 2019, 'Problematic sexual behaviour in children', *Journal of Pediatric Health Care*, vol. 33, no. 3, pp. 323–331, <https://doi.org/10.1016/j.pedhc.2018.11.002>.

Mojica, A 2017, *FBI issues sobering statistics on child pornography in the United States' dark web*, Fox 17, Nashville, April 17, viewed 1 January 2020, <https://fox17.com/news/local/fbi-issues-sobering-statistics-on-child-pornography-in-the-united-states-dark-web>.

Mullighan, E 2008, *Children in state care commission of inquiry: Allegations of sexual abuse and death from criminal conduct*, Adelaide, <www.childprotection.sa.gov.au/__data/assets/pdf_file/0011/107201/children-in-state-care-commission-of-inquiry-introducation.pdf>.

132 Conclusion

Murphy, K 2016, 'Coalition to unveil carve-up of $30m in domestic violence legal assistance', *The Guardian*, October 28, viewed 1 January 2020, <www.theguardian.com/society/2016/oct/28/coalition-to-unveil-carve-up-of-30m-in-domestic-violence-legal-assistance>.

New South Wales Legislative Council: General Purpose Standing Committee 2017, no. 2, *Child protection*, Sydney, <www.parliament.nsw.gov.au/lcdocs/inquiries/2396/Final%20report%20-%20Child%20protection.pdf>.

Nyland, M 2016, *The life they deserve: Child protection systems royal commission report*, SA Government, Adelaide, <https://agdsa.govcms.gov.au/sites/default/files/complete_report_child_protection_systems_royal_commission_report.pdf?acsf_files_redirect>.

O'Halloran, P 2011, *Final report: Select committee on child protection*, Parliament of Tasmania, Select Committee on Child Protection, Hobart, <www.parliament.tas.gov.au/ctee/House/childprotection.htm>.

Perry, BD 2005, *Maltreatment and the developing child: How early childhood experience shapes child and culture*, The Centre for Children and Families in the Justice System, London, viewed 1 January 2020, <https://childtrauma.org/wp-content/uploads/2013/11/McCainLecture_Perry.pdf>.

Perry, BD 2020, 'Emotional development: Creating an emotionally safe classroom', *Scholastic.com*, viewed 8 January 2020, <www.scholastic.com/teachers/articles/teaching-content/emotional-development-creating-emotionally-safe-classroom/>.

Royal Commission into Institutional Responses to Child Sexual Abuse 2017a, *Final report: Preface and executive summary*, Attorney General's Department, Canberra, <www.childabuseroyalcommission.gov.au/sites/default/files/final_report_-_preface_and_executive_summary.pdf>.

Royal Commission into Institutional Responses to Child Sexual Abuse 2017b, *Final report: Children with harmful sexual behaviours*, vol. 10, Attorney General's Department, Canberra, <www.childabuseroyalcommission.gov.au/sites/default/files/final_report_-_volume_10_children_with_harmful_sexual_behaviours.pdf>.

Schell, B, Vargas, M, Patrick, M, Hung, CK & Rueda, L 2007, 'Cyber child pornography: A review paper of the social and legal issues and remedies – and a proposed technological solution', *Aggression and Violent Behavior*, vol. 12, no. 1, pp. 45–63.

Senate Community Affairs Reference Committee 2001, *Lost innocence: Righting the record: Report on child migration*, Canberra, <www.aph.gov.au/Parliamentary_Business/Committees/Senate/Community_Affairs/completed_inquiries/1999-02/child_migrat/report/index.htm>.

Senate Community Affairs Reference Committee 2004, *Forgotten Australians: Report on Australians who experienced institutional or out-of-home care as children*, Canberra, <www.aph.gov.au/Parliamentary_Business/Committees/Senate/Community_Affairs/Completed_inquiries/2004-07/inst_care/report/index>.

Smith, TJ, Lindsey, RA, Bohora, S & Silovsky, JS 2019, 'Predictors of intrusive sexual behaviors in preschool-aged children', *Journal of Sex Research*, vol. 56 no. 2, pp. 229–238.

Streeck-Fischer, A & van der Kolk, B 2000, 'Down will come baby, cradle and all: Diagnostic and therapeutic implications of chronic trauma on child development', *Australian and New Zealand Journal Psychiatry*, vol. 34, no. 6, pp. 903–918, <https://doi.org/10.1080/000486700265>.

Victoria Parliament Family & Community Development Committee 2013, *Betrayal of trust: Inquiry into the handling of child abuse by religious and other non-government organisations*, Victoria Parliament, Melbourne.

Westlake, B, Bouchard, M, Frank, R & Fraser, S 2012, 'Comparing methods for detecting child exploitation content online', *European Intelligence and Security Informatics Conference*, <https://doi.org/10.1109/EISIC.2012.25>.

Wild, R & Anderson, P 2007, *Ampe akelyernemane meke mekarle: 'little children are sacred': Report of the Northern Territory board of inquiry into the protection of Aboriginal children from sexual abuse*, Northern Territory Government, Darwin, <www.inquirysaac.nt.gov.au/pdf/bipacsa_final_report.pdf>.

Index

Note: Page numbers in *italics* indicate a figure and page numbers in **bold** indicate a table on the corresponding page.

abstinence 3
abuse: effects of 44, 52; emotional 23, 51–52, 65, 122; physical 51–52, 75, 101; sexual (*see* sexual abuse); victims of 39, 41–42, 51–52, 53; violence, domestic 45, 49, 51–52, 65, 75, 79
Adverse Childhood Experiences project 39
Anangu Pitjantjatjara Yankunytjatjara Lands of Aboriginal peoples 103
anxiety 41–42, 44–45
Ariès, Philippe 2
attention-deficit/hyperactivity disorder (ADHD) 45
Australian Childhood Foundation 29, 41
Australia eSafety Commissioner 106
Australian Bureau of Statistics 25
Australian Child Protection Offender Reporting scheme 62
Australian Institute of Family Studies 5
Australian Institute of Health and Welfare: *Child protection 2017–18* 116; process managing 65

Baker, Amy J.L. 26
Bard, D. 27
Barter, Christine 4
BBC Freedom of Information: sexual offense, significant rise in reporting 26, 31

Berridge, David 4
Betrayal of trust report, Victoria 122
Big Talk Education 31
Bohora, Som 50
Bray, Chris 90
Briggs, Freda 6, 54, 56, 75, 108
Bromfield, Leah 87
Bronfenbrenner's Bio-Ecological System Theory 8, 99, *100*
bullying 76, 102
Burton, David L. 117

Carnes, Connie N. 109
child: abuse, emotional 23, 52, 65, 122; abuse, physical 52, 75, 101, 122; abuse, sexual 16, 23–24, 61; harmful sexual behavior 23; maltreatment of 24, 27, 49–50, 54, 102–104, 107, 110 (*see also* maltreatment, increase in); neglect 45, 50–53, 56–57, 75, 102, 110, 122; safety, parental measures 108; sex offenders 103–104
childcare services 115, 117
child protection: behaviours, identifying and reporting 107–108, 110, 115; laws, abuse as categorized 52, 63, 103, 104; legislation 29; notifications, handling of 119; services 116–117, 118, 120, 128; system 23, 50 120–121, 126; training, resources for 17
child sexual abuse (CSA) 52

Child Sexual Behavior Inventory (CSBI) 26
childhood: innocence, protecting 3; sexual abuse 29, 41; sexual behaviour 4, 6, 12, 14, 31, 39, 76; social construct, as expressed view 2; trauma, impact of 42, 50
Childline 26
children: behaviour change, positive 63; behaviour, cognitive development of 5, 7, 50, 57, 84; boys, as more assertive 101; categorizing, as harmful 4; characteristics, of person 99, *100*, 101; consent, age of 2, 24, 61; disabilities, intellectual 54–55, 57, 101–102, 125; environment, as primary influence for development 53, 100, 103; exploitation of 49, 56, 63, 104–107, 123–124, 129; identity formation and 45; indigenous, child protection services and 103, 116, 121; miniature adults, seen as 2; self-efficacy, developing 92; sexual development 3, 12–13, 98, 123; sexual expression, as harmful 6–7, 13, 15–16, 24, 30–31; support and recovery 8, 67, 71, 76–80, 83, 93; temperament, as factor 99–100, 101
Children and Young People (Safety) Act 2017 (SA) 65
chronosystem 104
Cicchetti, Dante 99, 102
coercive violence, exposure to 126
cognitive behaviour therapy 84–85
Commission of Inquiry 118
Commonwealth Criminal Code Act 1995 63
consent 24, 61
Cook, Alexandra 40

Darwin, Charles 3
data collection, techniques of 24
Davies, Hobart W. 50
Debelle Royal Commission 119
DeLamater, John 3
depression 39, 41, 45
diseases, as related to sexual abuse 43
domestic violence 45, 49, 52, 65, 75, 79
Donisch, Katelyn 90

early intervention, as successful 86, 89, 119–120
education, setting and harmful sexual behaviour 24, 30–31, 52, 71, 76, 83–84, 94; *see also* educators
educators: discomfort in expression 74; guidelines, developed for 12, 94; relationship building strategies 93; reporting and responding 80, 89, 109–110; role of, as significant 83; sexual behaviour, ability to recognize typical 73; stress, trauma exposure 79; training, as insufficient and inconsistent 71–72, 75–76, 77–78; training, on-demand access desired 78, 106–107
Elkovitch, Natasha 101
Elliot, Ann N. 109
exosystem 102
Ey, Lesley-anne 78, 87

family: behaviours, as violent 53, 65, 103–104, 110, 116–117, 122–125; boundaries, as not set 53; dynamics 53; education, as awareness for safety 107; parent involvement, child safety 26, 108; parenting, as neglectful 52–53, 56–57; relationships 13, 53
family law: child protection and 7, 61–62, 103–104, 128; risk assessment 64
Family Law Act (1975) 64
fear: consequences of 24, 98, 108; feelings of 44, 92, 126; responses 42
Feher, Eleonora 50
Felitti, Vincent J. 39
Finkelhor, David 30
Fisher, Cate 41
flashing, of genitals 18, 30
Flood, Michael 5, 56, 105
Florida Department of Child and Family Services 26
Friedrich, William N. 3, 26, 50

Gagnon, John H. 13
Gaskill, Richard L. 40
gender identity 14
gender role: adult 14; environment as influence of 13–14, 15, 73

Index

Gewirtz, Abigail 90
girls: exploitation of 55–56, 101, 105; maturation, beginning of 15, 16; sexual behaviours of 27–28, 30; treated as different 13–14; vulnerable, as needing protection 3, 117
Goldsmith, Alexandra 41
Grant, Jan 116, 117

Hamby, Sherry 30
harmful sexual behaviour (HSB) 71, 76, 83; awareness, as limited 98; causes, as search for 7, 45, 77, 99; challenges arising from 98, 104, 110, 115, 125–127; characteristics in children 49; coercion/aggression 18–19, 76, 109, 121–122; defined 4, 74; early intervention and 86, 89, 119–120; effects of 7, 38–39, **40**, 45; identifying 55, 78–79, 98, 102, 103; interpersonal 18, 45, 91, 110, 127; language, as descriptive of 12; managing 80, 98; peer-on-peer 18–19, 26, 31; preventing 86, 98–99, 104, 106–108; responses to 83, 87–88, 109–110; secrecy 18, 74, 109; support services for 85, **85**, 86, 88–89; therapies for 84–85
Hecht, DB 27
Hurcombe, Rachel 41

indecent acts 77
injuries, caused from sexual abuse 42–43
internet, online exposure and 105, 123–124
intrusive sexual behaviours (ISB) 50–51

Johnson, Toni Cavanagh 26

Keeping safe: Child protection curriculum 107, 108
Kershaw, Reece 123
Kilbourne, Jean 13
Krone, Tony 124

laws, Australian: child protection 104; child protection systems 62, 64, 65, 66; consent, age of 61, 63; *doli incapax* 63; educators, responsibilities of 65; family, conflicting and damaging 103; reporting, case overload problems 67
Layton Report 118
Levin, Diane E. 13
Lindsey, Rebecca A. 50
Little children are sacred report 120
Lloyd, Jenny 89, 93, 94
Lynch, Michael 99

macrosystem 103
maltreatment: difficult to define 24; increase in 116–118, 120, 125–129; reducing rates of 117, 128
McCoole, Shannon 119, 123
McHale, Susan M. 104
McInnes, Elspeth 78
McVeity, Michael 108
media, role of in shaping attitudes 5, 13, 55–56, 104–106
mental health: disorders associated with sexual abuse **40**, 41; services, as mainstream 86, 88, 90
Mesman, Glenn R. 14
mesosystem 102
morality 3
Moran, Claire 73
multisystemic therapy 84
music videos, as sexually explicit 105

National Center for Missing and Exploited Children (NCMEC) 129
National Community Attitudes towards Violence Against Women Survey (NCAS) 2017 104
National Society for the Prevention of Cruelty to Children (NSPCC) 26
New South Wales Department of Education: *Child protection policy: Responding to and reporting students at risk of harm* 76
Niec, Larissa N. 27
Northern Territory: abuse reporting requirements 65, 75; *Guidelines: Sexual behaviour in children* 77; *Little children are sacred* report 120–121
Nyland, Margaret 119

Office of Juvenile Justice and
Delinquency Prevention 25
Ormrod, Richard K. 30

parental substance abuse 39, 45, 79
*Passports Legislation Amendment
(Overseas Travel by Child Sex
Offenders) Act 2017* 63
peer support 13, 67, 94, 98
perpetrator: abuser as 39, 63, 75, 80, 110; labelling, as language 4, 16, 18, 45, 118
Perry, Bruce D. 40, 92
Pintello, Denise 109
pornography: exploitation of children and 115, 123–124, 128–129; exposure to on behaviours 4–5, 8, 49, 54; internet, exposure to 56–57, 105, 123; rapid growth of 123–124
post-traumatic stress disorder (PTSD) 41, 50
PRACTICE, response guideline for educators 90–91
prostitution 2, 25
proximal processes 99–100
puberty 2–3, 16, 94–95

Queensland Department of Education: *Student protection guidelines* 77

rape 25, 30, 43, 74, 77
relationships: healthy, as having 31, 94–95, 107; interpersonal 38, 39, 41–42, 45, 104; parent/child, familial 13, 53, 101, 102, 103, 128; peer, developing normal 54, 67, 74, 90–91, 110; perpetrators, as child's 39, 109
reporting, as mandatory 62–63, 65, 67, 72, 77
reproduction, sexual 3, 14–15, 74
residential care, as higher risk for abuse 26, 111
Rigney, Lester Irabinna 78
Rosa, Maria Edinete 100
Royal Commission into Institutional Responses to Child Sexual Abuse: harmful sexual behaviours and children 17, 29, 31; out-of-home care 122–123; policies and procedures 94; report findings, as disturbing 122, 125; survivor statistics 39

schools: avoidance, as indicator of abuse 44–45; environment, as risk factor 19, 26, 29–32, 93; responsibility, as legal 7–8, 26, 61, 65–66; sex education and 3 (*see also* sex education); teachers, need to be informed (*see* educators)
Senate Community Affairs Reference Committee: *Forgotten Australians* inquiry 121–122; *Lost innocence* report 121
sex education 3, 31, 54, 94–95, 123
sex offenders: children, as targets 54, 63–64; children, labelled as 24; prosecution of, as difficult 62
sex organs 4, 15
sexual abuse: cases, 2015–16 (Australia) 6; counselling for peer-on-peer abuse 26; health costs, related to 39, 42–43; homelessness and 44; lasting effects of 43; mental illness and 39, 41; non-contact 28; peer-on-peer 26, 30, 72, 76; psychological impacts of 44; rise in 5–6; risk factors 44–45, 50; trauma and (*see* trauma, symptoms of exposure to)
sexual assault: children, by other children 24–25, 30–31, 72; criminal conviction, of children 25, 46, 55; economic cost of 38
sexual behaviour: age appropriate 17, 32, 57, 76–77, 98, 107, 124; aggressive 4–5, 16–17, 27, 41, 51; attitudes of 1, 4, 57, 103–105; concerning 3, 6, 12, 17–18, 20, 32, 38, 77; education setting 30, 43–44, 71; intrusive 17, 28, 50, 52; labels of 4; masturbation and 17–18, 74, 117; pornography and 74 (*see also* pornography); reportable, as mandatory 63 (*see also* educators); risk factors, for developing 45, 51, 53, 55, 102, 124; signifiers, as mainstream 4–5; teenagers, typical signs of 74–75

Index

sexual behaviour problems (SBP) 52
sexual characteristics 14–15
sexual crime 7, 32, 61
sexual development: age appropriate 124; in children 13–14; dysfunctional 1; expression of 3, 13; healthy 14, 16, 85; infancy, as beginning in 13; natural 6; physiological, primary and hormonal 14–15; puberty, as sexual milestone 2; social influences 13; typical, as defined 6, 12, 15, 17, 28, 87
sexual exploitation 2, 7, 45, 117, 121, 128
sexual harassment 30
sexual reactions 3
sexual reproduction organs 74
Shattuck, Anne 30
Silovsky, Jane 27, 50
Simon, William 13
Smith, Russell G. 124
Smith, Tyler J. 50
Soares, Claire 41
social scripting 13
social stigma 45
South Australian Child Protection Systems Royal Commission 72
South Australia's Department for Education: *Responding to problem sexual behaviour in children and young people: Guidelines for staff in education and care settings* 76, 87, 117
Staiger, Petra Karin 4
Streeck-Fischer, Annette 50
suicide, abuse related 41

technologies, developments in, as contributing to increased sexual activity 5
'traffic lights' resource material 73

trauma: behaviours from, as confusing 92; chronic 45; complex 40, 52, 57, 102, 104, 110, 116, 126; mental illness and 41; physical health, effects on 42–43; relationships affected by 41; sexual identity and 42; symptoms of exposure to 39
trauma informed practice 90
True Relationships and Reproductive Health: *Sexual behaviours in children and young people* 77
Tucci, Joe, Dr 29
Tudge, Jonathan 100
Turner, Heather A. 30

underreported, significantly 24, 124

van der Kolk, Bessel A. 50
victims, child abuse 42, 44, 62, 72, 120, 126
Victoria: *Identifying and responding to student sexual offending* 77
Victorian Parliament Family and Community Development Committee: *Betrayal of trust: Inquiry into the handling of child abuse by religious and other non-government organisations* report 121
violent crimes, reported as 25

Western Australian Education Department 77
women, violence against 104, 128
Worthman, Carol 14
Wright, John 50
Wunsch, Angela 73

youth justice 63, 68n2
Yuen, Angel 92

Zuravin, Susan 109

For Product Safety Concerns and Information please contact our EU representative GPSR@taylorandfrancis.com
Taylor & Francis Verlag GmbH, Kaufingerstraße 24, 80331 München, Germany

www.ingramcontent.com/pod-product-compliance
Lightning Source LLC
Chambersburg PA
CBHW070738230426
43669CB00014B/2492